Neuropsychological Rehabilitation

Neuropsychological Rehabilitation

A Resource for Group-Based Education and Intervention

Andrew J. Champion

Health Psychology Department, Gloucestershire Royal Hospital

John Wiley & Sons, Ltd

MT

Other Wiley Editorial Offices

John Wiley & Sons Inc., 111 River Street, Hoboken, NJ 07030, USA

Jossey-Bass, 989 Market Street, San Francisco, CA 94103-1741, USA

Wiley-VCH Verlag GmbH, Boschstr. 12, D-69469 Weinheim, Germany

John Wiley & Sons Australia Ltd, 42 McDougall Street, Milton, Queensland 4064, Australia

John Wiley & Sons (Asia) Pte Ltd, 2 Clementi Loop 02-01, Jin Xing Distripark, Singapore 129809

John Wiley & Sons Canada Ltd, 6045 Freemont Blvd, Mississauga, ONT, Canada L5R 4J3

Wiley also publishes its books in a variety of electronic formats. Some content that appears in print may not be available
in electronic books.

Library of Congress Cataloging-in-Publication Data

Champion, A. J.
    Neuropsychological rehabilitation : a resource for group-based education and intervention/A.J. Champion.
        p. cm.
    Includes bibliographical references and index.
    ISBN-13: 978-0-470-02639-7 (pbk. : alk. paper)
    ISBN-10: 0-470-02639-1 (pbk. : alk. paper
  1. Brain damage–Patients–Rehabilitation. 2. Clinical neuropsychology. I. Title.
    [DNLM: 1. Nervous System Diseases–rehabilitation. 2. Rehabilitation–methods. WL 140 C452n 2006]
    RC387.5.C52 2006
    617.4'810443–dc22

                                                              2006010701

British Library Cataloguing in Publication Data

A catalogue record for this book is available from the British Library
ISBN-13: 978-0-470-02639-7 (pbk)
ISBN-10: 0-470-02639-1 (pbk)

Typeset in 11/13 pt Times by Thomson Digital
Printed and bound in Great Britain by Antony Rowe, Chippenham, Wiltshire
This book is printed on acid-free paper responsibly manufactured from sustainable forestry
in which at least two trees are planted for each one used for paper production.

4/11/07

Contents

About the Author

Dr Andrew Champion has worked in NHS inpatient and outpatient neuro-rehabilitation settings since qualifying as a clinical psychologist in 2001, most recently working as part of a multidisciplinary Head Injury Team and contributing to the work of inpatient and community stroke services. As well as specialising in the assessment and subsequent rehabilitation of people who experience acquired brain injury, Dr Champion teaches on these topics at both doctoral and postdoctoral diploma level, and is a Full Practitioner member of the British Psychological Society's Division of Neuropsychology.

Acknowledgements

The author would like to express how privileged he feels to have worked alongside so many dedicated and caring professionals during a decade of working in the National Health Service. It is through their efforts that the quality of care received by so many people in need of neuro-rehabilitation is as high as it is.

Thanks are due to the staff and patients of the Frank Cooksey Rehabilitation Unit at King's College Hospital, London, where the materials produced in this book first began to be developed. Fleur Coughlan and Kate Wright were instrumental in initiating group work on this unit. Particular mention must go to Andrew McCarthy and Barbara O'Sullivan for their unique contributions to the running of the Frank Cooksey Rehabilitation Unit.

Thanks must go to the Health Psychology Department at Gloucestershire Royal Hospital, and particularly to the Head Injury team managed by Dr Aileen Thomson for their encouragement regarding the continued development and running of neuro-rehabilitation programmes.

The author would like to thank his family and God for their unconditional love and support.

Chapter 1

Information Provision in Neuro-rehabilitation

For me, information is absolutely the most important thing. No-one told me, or my family, about the radical emotional and behavioural changes that a brain injury would force on me.

(Headway: the Brain Injury Association, 2005)

While for many people involved in the field of brain injury – professionals, carers and patients alike – it seems intuitively correct that the provision of information relating to such a sudden and potentially life-changing event should be an important part of after-care, in today's evidence-based and financially restricted context for clinical practice, this falls far short of constituting a sufficient rationale for investing resources such as healthcare professionals' time and room space (such a precious resource in so many NHS settings) into group-based education interventions. An indication of how low down the list of priorities systematic information provision often falls is provided by the results of a recent survey of approximately 100 healthcare professionals (including nurses, neurologists and therapists) working with people who have neurological conditions. In only one per cent of the neurological settings investigated were any financial resources available for education and information interventions (Brain and Spine Foundation, 2005).

This chapter is intended to summarise the evidence-base supporting such a use of resources, with the aim of assisting the practising clinician to justify the implementation of group-based education and rehabilitation sessions to those in the management hierarchy who may hold sway. This aim has an effective ally in the recently produced *National Service Framework for Long-term Conditions* (Department of Health, 2005), and this document will be considered in some depth.

Information provision in neurological settings

Irrespective of the nature of an individual's condition, there are established findings suggesting that equipping people with information relating to their health condition has beneficial effects. In a concise overview of such findings, Barton, Levene, Kladakis and Butterworth (2002) cite studies spanning the past few decades. Ley (1988) notes that increasing patients' knowledge is associated with increased adherence to health regimes, as well as with increased patient satisfaction. Furthermore, adjustment to illness has been linked with increasing patients' access to relevant information (Reynolds, 1978).

Neurological conditions are no exception to this. Morrison, Johnston, MacWalter and Pollard (1998) evaluated a workbook-based intervention and found that such an educational approach was associated with significantly reduced levels of depression and anxiety following stroke, while Kelly-Hayes and Paige (1995) linked the provision of information relating to stroke with strengthened social support systems.

Despite the evidence relating to the benefits of providing information to patients with neurological conditions, it is apparent that the provision of such information is often lacking in either its quantity or in the way that it is presented. Barton et al. (2002) identify two potentially problematic elements to the provision of information to people who have had a stroke, in that either health professionals do not communicate the relevant information, or that it is presented in such a way that the people who have had a stroke are not able to assimilate it. In the Brain and Spine Foundation's (2005) study, a major reason given by health professionals as to why they were often unable to provide information regarding people's conditions was shortage of time, a situation that will be familiar to the majority of healthcare professionals in the NHS. One hope for the material provided in the following chapters is that the time-consuming preparation stage of structured information provision will be shortened considerably by the collation of information and resources into one volume.

Barton et al. (2002) go on to cite two studies to demonstrate their assertion that there are inadequacies in the quantity or the nature of information provision in settings that have a neuro-rehabilitation component. Gariballa et al. (1996) investigated patients who had either had a stroke or had ischaemic heart disease, and found that 86% of the people in their sample were unable to recall receiving any information or advice regarding their condition during the time that they were in hospital. The conclusion was that the methods of providing the information were not proving successful. Hanger and Mulley (1993) examined the nature of enquiries received by the UK Stroke association over a period of four months, and found that almost a quarter of all enquiries related to fundamental information about stroke that could or should have been provided by health professionals involved in the care of the individuals concerned. The conclusion, as above, was that either information was not being given to patients and their relatives/carers, or that it was not being given in an accessible form.

Further weight is added to these concerns from the findings of a Cochrane review carried out by Forster et al. (2002), which related to information provision for stroke patients and their caregivers. Forster et al. begin by acknowledging that provision of information and advice relating to stroke is recommended as a central aspect of care, citing the King's Fund (1988) and HMSO (1999). Despite this, they contend that the level of understanding of their condition remains poor in patients who have had a stroke, using a number of studies to support this claim. For example, Wellwood, Dennis and Warlow (1994) surveyed UK patients who had recently been discharged from hospital following a stroke and found that approximately one in four was unable to describe the difference between a stroke and a heart attack. Similarly, Drummond, Lincoln and Juby (1996) found that approximately a quarter of patients discharged from a stroke unit were unaware that a stroke involved damage to the brain.

Forster et al.'s (2002) review highlights some of the benefits of information provision, including improved quality of care after discharge from hospital following information provision to carers (Evans, Bishop & Haselkorn, 1991) and compliance with secondary prevention (O'Mahoney, Rodgers, Thomson, Dobson & James, 1997).

One finding from Forster et al.'s (2002) Cochrane review is that information provision in the context of educational sessions does improve knowledge and is more effective than information provision without the educational session component (for example, issuing leaflets to patients). Although Forster et al. (2002) did not conclude that information provision had an effect on mood for patients or carers, more recently Young (2004) evaluated the provision of a short educational programme for carers using a randomised controlled trial, and concluded that it was associated with a significantly greater reduction in anxiety levels. The emphatic opinion espoused in this study is that patient education is a crucial element in the management of chronic disease (Young, 2004).

Clearly the presence of cognitive impairment is a challenge to effective communication that is particularly relevant to neurological conditions. If individuals lack insight into some aspects of their condition or its consequences, then this can pose a major obstacle to any rehabilitation attempts. If this is the case, then the focus of education about a condition can be shifted towards the family/carers of the individual. It is also becoming increasingly recognised that family members and carers should be given information about the condition and any associated difficulties; indeed this is specifically referred to in the National Service Framework for people with long-term neurological conditions (Department of Health, 2005).

Family and carers

Family members are the most common providers of ongoing care for people who experience a brain injury (Jacobs, 1988, cited in Hayes & Coetzer, 2003). Liamaki and Bach (2003) considered the utility of group-based intervention with the carers of brain-injured relatives, focusing on the qualitative feedback that they received from their group of six attendees. The three main benefits that were highlighted related to normalisation of their experience, validation of the burden of caring and their attempts to cope with difficulties, and the knowledge that there were avenues of support available.

It has been established that one of the most important perceived needs of family members and carers of people with brain injury is for accessible, clear information (Sinnakaruppan & Williams, 2001, cited in Hayes & Coetzer, 2003). More generally, carers tend to report that two elements of information provision are of most value to them; namely, information about the nature of the condition itself, and information about how to obtain support (Zarit & Edwards, 1999). As regards information pertaining to the condition, it is a robust finding that cognitive, emotional and behavioural changes have the most impact on carer burden (e.g. Oddy, Humphrey & Uttley, 1978; Knight, Devereux & Godfrey, 1998), and this tallies exactly with the content of the sessions included in the session plans described in the following chapters. Knight et al. (1998) go on to report some benefits of systematic education programmes for family members of people with traumatic brain injury in terms of their understanding and subsequent management of ongoing difficulties. Crucially Knight et al. (1998, p. 479) conclude that 'where carers are confident in their ability to cope, burden is reduced'. Providing understanding and strategies to help manage the cognitive and emotional changes is an essential part of increasing carers' perceived ability to cope.

The national service framework for long-term conditions[1]

The National Service Framework for Long-term Conditions (NSF-LTC) has a particular focus on people with neurological conditions and one of its intended outcomes is to improve health outcomes by bringing about systematic approaches to the delivery of treatment and care. It consists of 11 'quality requirements', and the very first of these is of great relevance to the provision of information to those with neurological conditions. This quality requirement is headed 'a person-centred service', and is described as being an essential prerequisite for the remaining 10 quality requirements. 'Providing information' is mentioned specifically as a key element of the first quality requirement under a heading of 'improving services' (Department of Health, 2005, p.13). A second area in which the NSF-LTC refers specifically to the provision of information is in quality requirement 10, in which 'the need to offer information, advice and support to families and carers' is emphasised (Department of Health, 2005, p.17).

In the expanded notes relating to quality requirement one (QR1), the NSF-LTC cites two publications based on expert professional and/or expert service user evidence, and one randomised controlled trial, to support its statement that 'providing good information and education benefits the person by improving opportunities for choice and levels of independence and can reduce consultation rates' (Department of Health, 2005, p.22). Two of the three publications cited relate to 'patients' in general rather than to specifically neurological populations (Department of Health, 2001; 2004), while the third (the randomised controlled trial) relates to the provision of written information in the form of a booklet for patients experiencing back pain (Roland & Dixon, 1989).

It is stressed that, in order for such input to be effective, it must be designed and provided in a way that renders it accessible to the target population. At this point, the NSF-LTC highlights the ongoing need for staff throughout the disciplines and at varying levels of experience to undergo training in order to communicate effectively with people who may have cognitive impairments, citing as support the NICE (2003) National Clinical Guidelines for Multiple Sclerosis. This recommendation supports the provision of information regarding the consequences of brain injury to healthcare professionals, a third intended population (in addition to service users and their families/carers) who may benefit from structured information provision, for example in the form of attendance at a series of group sessions.

The NSF-LTC suggests that a range of formats is beneficial when presenting information for people with neurological conditions and their carers. The advantage of a group setting (for those who are able to engage in such a setting effectively) is that such a range is pos-

[1]Crown copyright material is reproduced with the permission of the Controller of HMSO and the Queen's Printer for Scotland.

sible. Group settings lend themselves well to the use of visual aids, including prepared slides and handouts containing written summaries, while other accessible formats will include functional examples generated by other attendees, demonstration and rehearsal of particular strategies within the sessions, as well as the spoken verbal content of the session.

The NSF-LTC acknowledges the importance of the timing of information provision. While this is considered in more depth in Chapter 2, there is some consensus that information provision in the post-acute time period is recommended (e.g. Barton et al., 2002). The notion that there is a 'window of opportunity' for information provision is one that can be particularly compelling when seeking to provide such input in, for example, an inpatient post-acute rehabilitation setting.

The first quality requirement identifies a range of 'markers', which serve as objective indices of whether or not good practice is being observed. One such marker is that 'people receive timely . . . information . . . on the condition and how best to manage it' (Department of Health, 2005, p.23), and this is supported by, among other publications, a systematic review relating to the information and counselling needs of people with epilepsy (Couldridge, Kendall & March, 2001). A second marker is that 'people with long-term neurological conditions and their carers can access education and self-management programmes' (Department of Health, 2005, p. 23), a marker based on a range of quantitative and qualitative research (e.g. Darragh, Sample & Krieger, 2001; O'Hara, Cadbury, De & Ide, 2002).

The central importance of providing information is highlighted by the fact that QR1 is referred back to throughout the other 10 quality requirements. For example, in QR2 (which relates to 'early recognition, prompt diagnosis and treatment') it is stated explicitly that inherent within receiving a diagnosis of a long-term condition, 'people need information about their condition and an opportunity to talk through the implications for them' (Department of Health, 2005, p.25), and attendance at courses run by healthcare professionals is included as an example of such good practice. The importance of 'specialist advice from people who understand their condition' is mentioned, with particular reference to conditions including multiple sclerosis, for which input from specialist nurses has been well documented in terms of clinical and cost effectiveness (e.g. Johnson, Smith & Goldstone, 2001).

QR3 deals with emergency and acute management, a stage in which structured provision of information regarding long-term consequences is less relevant, although it is of note that even at this stage there is an acknowledgement that staff need to be well-informed about conditions, and also that patients and their families are to be kept informed about the current condition, with care taken to avoid breakdowns in communication, particularly if the patient is transferred between settings.

QR4, dealing as it does with 'early and specialist rehabilitation' cites references that recommend the provision of information (e.g. Turner-Stokes, 2003), and clearly emphasises the utility of a multidisciplinary approach. Having more than one professional discipline present in structured group settings has a number of benefits (see Chapter 2), which overlap with the generation of a cohesive multidisciplinary goal-driven approach to an individual's rehabilitation.

QR5 focuses on 'community rehabilitation and support'. Essentially, this quality requirement demands that patients can access continued rehabilitation, advice and support after their discharge from an inpatient setting, with a view to enhancing independent living. The range of areas which this should cover is summarised in the NSF-LTC as including 'physical, emotional, psychological and social' (Department of Health, 2005, p. 35), and evidence is cited linking decreased community participation with a range of neurological conditions, including stroke (Drummond, 1990), head injury (Oddy, Coughlan, Tyerman & Jenkins, 1985) and spinal injury (Tasienski et al., 2000). Other consequences that can arise if some or all of these needs are not addressed are highlighted, including social isolation, anxiety and depression. Studies cited in the NSF-LTC relate these sequelae to various conditions including spinal cord injury (Kennedy & Rogers, 2000), multiple sclerosis (Nicholl, Lincoln, Francis & Stephan, 2001) and Parkinson's disease (Raskin et al., 1990). Crucially for the provision of structured condition-related information in this setting, it has been demonstrated that improved adjustment to a condition 'lessens the burden on carers and reliance on services, prevents unnecessary hospital admissions and can lead to substantial savings over the long term' (Department of Health, 2005, p.35). The last two elements from this statement in particular are likely to be of use when attempting to access resources to run structured multidisciplinary patient information groups, and the NSF-LTC refers particularly to a study by Malec, Smigielski, Depompolo & Thompson (1993) in justifying this stance.

Within QR5 there is further support for running courses aimed at increasing the expertise of healthcare professionals, particularly generic community teams. Providing knowledge relating to some of the consequences of long-term neurological conditions to these professionals is described as a 'key issue' in developing 'responsive and high quality rehabilitation in the community' (Department of Health, 2005, p.36).

Furthermore, mention is made of the need to provide information and education alongside practical advice and skills to people with neurological conditions, their family and their carers. Specific publications are cited that refer to conditions including stroke (Kersten, Low, Ashburn, George & McLellan, 2002), spinal cord injury (Boschen, Tonack & Gargaro, 2003), and multiple sclerosis (Freeman et al., 2002). One of the evidence-based markers of good practice for QR5 is that people with a long-term neurological condition, their family and carers will 'develop knowledge and skills to manage their condition' (Department of Health, 2005, p.38). This is supported by three studies relating to acquired brain injury; one comprises a two-year follow-up relating to social adjustment (Weddell et al., 1980), while the second and third relate to evaluation of community-based rehabilitation (Pace et al., 1999; Powell, Heslin & Greenwood, 2002), the most recent being a randomised controlled trial (Powell et al., 2002).

QR6 relates to vocational rehabilitation. In practice, for many people with long-term neurological conditions such as acquired brain injury, it is in the work setting that the impact of more subtle cognitive sequelae becomes apparent, as the workplace is often characterised by multiple demands and time pressures. Indeed, as Lezak (1995) notes, after a 'mild' head injury, which does not require an extended admission to hospital, but may lead to an individual taking a few days off work, it is not uncommon for some cognitive difficulties to remain undetected until the individual begins to challenge themselves

cognitively – often this means on returning to work where skills such as divided attention, prioritisation and flexible thinking are at a premium. Normalising such difficulties
and suggesting management strategies (both 'internal' and relating to environmental
modification) can equip people to reduce the impact of cognitive difficulties on their daily
work activities, and can facilitate productive discussions with employers regarding reasonable adjustments that can be made in the workplace. The long-term effectiveness of
providing such information early has been demonstrated in the literature relating to mild
head injury (e.g. King, 2003).

QR7 deals with the provision of equipment and accommodation, and incorporates assistive
technology to support independent living. While this encompasses sophisticated equipment
such as environmental modifications and communication aids that can have marked implications for quality of life, it must also cover the various 'cognitive prostheses', from diaries
to paging systems. For people to implement such strategies they need to be aware of them,
and also aware of the rationale for their utility, as would be predicted by the Theory of
Planned Behaviour (e.g. Ajzen, 1985). Once again, education about the nature of cognitive
deficits and information regarding rehabilitation strategies is a prerequisite for this.

Within QR8, which relates to 'providing personal care and support', there is an essential place for ensuring that – in whatever setting an individual may choose to live to meet
their ongoing needs – care staff are familiar with the range of difficulties that are common in long-term neurological conditions. Two 'key elements of successful home care'
(Department of Health, 2005, p. 48) related to the provision of information are explicitly
recommended in the NSF-LTC. Firstly, those who are providing the direct day-to-day
input should receive training in order that rehabilitation becomes inbuilt into an individual's
daily routine. Secondly, in a very similar recommendation, professionals in rehabilitation
should provide training in the needs of people with long-term neurological conditions.
While these two recommendations can seem somewhat duplicative, on closer reading it
seems that the first relates more to specific interventions that need to be maintained on a
daily basis for their benefit to be gained (such as wearing splints, or using a whiteboard),
while the second is intended to provide care staff with a broader understanding of the
rationale for some of the interventions recommended in order to facilitate understanding
of individual needs. The provision of such information (as would be provided by a structured
education/information package) is one of the evidence-based markers of good practice for
QR8.

QR9 is headed 'palliative care'. While specialist palliative care services emphasising
quality of life are well developed and implemented by a range of specialist professionals,
including nurses, social workers and hospice staff, some neurological conditions present
with specific features in their more advanced stages (e.g. cognitive impairment) that may
be less familiar to these staff. It is for this reason that QR9 suggests that in some situations, staff working in a palliative care setting may benefit from training regarding some
of the consequences of neurological conditions such as cognitive changes (e.g. Kite,
Jones & Tookman, 1999). Matters of capacity to make decisions can become particularly pertinent in palliative settings, and providing information relating to cognition to
those involved in such situations can be an important element in demystifying some of
this sensitive decision-making process.

QR10, 'supporting family and carers', is of particular relevance to information provision in neurological conditions, as well as often being crucial in the ongoing quality of life of an individual. It is a robust finding that, among the range of realistically distressing and exhausting changes with which a carer is faced on a daily basis, those that have the most impact tend to reflect changes in cognitive, emotional and behavioural functioning (e.g. Zarit & Edwards, 1999). The NSF-LTC cites a range of studies demonstrating this, including a 5-year review of relatives' experiences after head injury (Brooks, Campsie, Symington, Beattie & McKinlay, 1986), the psychological impact of motor neurone disease on patients and carers (Goldstein et al., 1998) and a study of over 300 patients and their relatives examining the impact of multiple sclerosis (Hakim et al., 2004).

Many of the common cognitive consequences of neurological conditions can easily be misinterpreted, and providing a non-blaming explanation for the presence of some behaviour changes can go some way towards reducing unnecessary friction in a relationship. Furthermore, providing some practical suggestions for ways in which some cognitive changes can be managed can engender some feeling of control over a situation in which it is all too easy to feel helpless (Knight et al., 1998).

The benefits of providing detailed information to families and carers regarding management of the specific condition has been demonstrated (Kalra et al., 2004). Two of the recommendations included in a list of actions that can reduce carers' stress levels and improve their quality of life involve the provision of training and intervention. The first, involving carers in implementation of a care plan, would require their training in, for example, memory management strategies. The second relates to the more general and timely provision of information about the condition and its effects, citing support from published work relating to, among others, the provision of information packs to the families of people who have had a stroke (Mant, Carter, Wade & Winner, 1998) and a study of the information needs of carers of adults diagnosed with epilepsy (Kendall, Thompson & Couldridge, 2004).

The final quality requirement, QR11, is entitled 'caring for people with neurological conditions in hospital or other health and social care settings'. Essentially, this is designed to ensure that, whatever the acute reason for treatment, an acknowledgement of the long-term condition is incorporated into the care that an individual receives. Of particular relevance in this context is the point raised that 'people who have behavioural, cognitive and/or communication problems (e.g. due to a brain injury) have particular needs of which staff may have little experience' (Department of Health, 2005, p. 59). The provision of training and advice for staff who find themselves in such a situation is one of the evidence-based markers of good practice for QR11, and similar recommendations are made in other guidelines for clinical practice (Royal College of Physicians, 1998; Turner-Stokes, 2003).

It is clear that the provision of information about the common consequences of neurological conditions can be seen as a fundamental requirement of implementing the NSF-LTC, and plays a part (to varying degrees) in each of the 11 quality requirements. Not only should improved clinical care and outcomes result from application of the NSF-LTC, but also services should fare well in terms of cost effectiveness. As NHS Trusts and local authorities will have to demonstrate that they are making progress towards achieving the 11 quality requirements, there is a good argument for suggesting that providing structured patient/carer/staff information sessions, which could be used as evidence of working towards several (if not all) of the quality requirements simultaneously, would be a good use of resources, and hence a good area in which to provide the necessary resources such as staffing, resources and equipment.

Conclusions

Information provision is often absent or ineffective after neurological insult, despite being highlighted as a need by service users, and despite being linked with a range of advantages (both clinical and financial). Timely provision of information is a recurring theme in the government's latest directive for guiding service provision, towards which all NHS trusts must aim. The following chapters are intended to aid this. The format adopted in the following chapters (i.e. initial sufficient information about a particular topic – such as attention or memory – to provide a rationale for the subsequent intervention suggestions included within the same session) has been shown to be effective using this particular material. Champion, Higbed, Jones and Thomson (2005) describe the use of the 'memory' material presented in Chapter 5 as a stand-alone session, which led to a statistically significant increase in attendees' use of memory strategies one month later, with the mean increase being two extra strategies being employed daily. Furthermore, one of the key advantages of group-based intervention was highlighted in this study, in that 85% of attendees who completed feedback forms responded to an open question asking for comments by indicating that they had found it helpful to meet other people with similar difficulties to their own (Champion et al., 2005). While much of the material presented in the following chapters is explicitly intended to normalise common consequences of neurological conditions, this effect of the shared experiences of the attendees themselves cannot be overstated.

Chapter 2

Before the First Session

This chapter is intended to serve as a prompt to some of the practical factors that will require consideration prior to running information sessions, whether this is a single-session stand-alone intervention (for example, a session for patients and their families about managing memory difficulties), or a series of six sessions considering a range of cognitive and emotional sequelae of neurological involvement. Many of these factors will be common sense to health professionals working in neuro-rehabilitation settings, but are included lest they be thought not worthy of mention. It is certainly the case that one of the major benefits of attending a group intervention derives from meeting other people with similar difficulties to one's own (e.g. Champion et al., 2005), but this advantage can be undone if the composition of the group is not given due attention.

Inclusion/exclusion criteria

For groups to which patients will be invited to attend, consideration needs to be given to any exclusion and inclusion criteria for attendees. Cognitive, behavioural, physical and emotional factors are important to be aware of in selecting potential attendees. By their nature, information/education groups tend to be largely verbally mediated, and as such may be inaccessible to patients with receptive dysphasia. They also require an ability to maintain concentration in a setting that can be distracting due to the presence of a number of other people. While to an extent this can be allowed for by the inclusion of at least one break within a session, and having more than one facilitator to take the lead, for some people with attention difficulties a group setting will be an inappropriate way to present information, and they are likely to benefit more from individual input. When considering potential attendees, not only the effects of the group setting on the individual should be considered, but also the effects of the individual on the group setting. Some of the features of executive dysfunction may be viewed as potentially prohibitive to engagement with a group setting; people who demonstrate verbal or other forms of disinhibition, or who have a tendency to perseverate on a particular theme, or who are experiencing marked emotional lability, may reduce the utility of the group setting for other attendees if their presentation disrupts the overall goal of sharing information for normalisation and practical management.

Physical characteristics also need consideration. Wheelchair users must be considered; if the room that is available is not on the ground floor, then there must be lift access to make their attendance practical, and the layout of the room needs to take into account the need to manoeuvre wheelchairs. Fatigue is very common in neurological conditions, and if an individual is currently not able to maintain alertness for an extended time then it may well be too early for them to benefit from a group setting. Continence is an important matter that will require discussion with the nursing staff and/or carers as to how this can be managed over the course of a session that might last for two hours; it is possible for this to be managed with the use of dual facilitators if one is trained in manual handling and the attendee needs only the assistance of one for toileting. Similarly, if an individual begins to experience pain or discomfort if they are seated in the same position for extended periods of time, then their ability to benefit from long group sessions is likely to be diminished. For some individuals and their families, the consideration of the presence of cognitive difficulties, let alone an explanation of their presence and constructive consideration of their management, is associated with a strength of emotional response which requires more tailored communication on an individual basis.

It will be apparent that the material in the following chapters relates more than anything else to acquired brain injury. The attempt has been to make the material broad-based enough to relate to a wide range of aetiologies, such that it is of relevance to individuals in need of neuro-rehabilitation rather than being condition-specific. It is likely to be less applicable to progressive conditions, although it is by no means the case that specific rehabilitation interventions have no place in, for example, the dementias (Moniz-Cook & Rusted, 2004).

Timing

It is clear from some of the factors mentioned already that there is an acute/post-acute period during which it is likely to be impractical for people to be able to engage with lengthy information-based sessions. Liamaki and Bach's (2003) sample of carers who attended information sessions indicated that their mean time from brain injury to attending group sessions (10.5 months) was too long and information would have been welcome sooner. Barton et al. (2002) conclude that the post-acute stage is the most effective stage at which to provide information in such a structured setting, although it is apparent that prior to this information should be provided as much as possible on an individual basis.

Facilitation

There are a number of advantages to dual facilitation. Some relate to the practicalities of managing a group of patients who have varying needs regarding, for example, mobility, continence or prompting to stay on task. If it becomes apparent that an attendee is not benefiting from the session, or is becoming upset, or some of the features of their presentation (such as disinhibition) are proving overly disruptive then having two facilitators can make it easier to deal with such matters with the least disruption. There is much evidence supporting a multidisciplinary approach to neuro-rehabilitation (Department of Health, 2005), and this is as true in information provision as it is in other aspects of rehabilitation. It is very important to try and make the information presented in the session as functional as it possibly can be; much of the information regarding cognition is unfamiliar to most people, and as such can seem very theoretical and unrelated to daily life unless it is linked clearly with practical examples. Professionals such as clinical psychologists, occupational therapists and speech and language therapists are ideally placed to do just this. The importance of using concrete examples is accentuated when running groups for patients who may well have cognitive impairments themselves, as one such impairment includes difficulty dealing with abstract concepts.

Environment and session structure

As mentioned above, it is important to take into consideration the fact that for many people with neurological conditions, fatigue and concentration have an impact on their ability to stay engaged with a session for extended periods. Hence, it is important to plan breaks within the sessions. This also allows for more informal interaction with individuals, who may wish to ask particular questions of the facilitators, or may wish to speak to other attendees about their situation.

While a group setting has some inherent distractions in the form of the presence of other people, some efforts can be made to reduce environmental distractions, by, for example, closing blinds/curtains, turning off any noisy equipment and considering which way the attendees will face bearing in mind the potential visual distractions within the room. By the nature of some of the attendees, some will have difficulties with remembering information, and so the provision of handouts is advisable; in Chapter 1, some of the shortfalls in information provision were clearly attributed to the manner in which information was presented rather than the lack of information provision, and it is vital to provide information in a way that takes into account the very difficulties with which people may be presenting. For the same reason, there are benefits to inviting the families/carers of individuals with neurological conditions to the sessions, as they are more likely to retain some of the information. The use of overheads has the advantage of providing a structure within which material is presented, which can be of use for individuals with executive difficulties, but can also prove invaluable for people who present with slowed information processing, as they may be able to appreciate the gist of the message even if some of the details are presented too quickly, a common difficulty even when those facilitating attempt to speak at a pace that will reduce this.

Open/closed groups

When planning a group that will run over a number of sessions, one fundamental decision is whether to have an 'open' group or a 'closed' group. Both have their advantages and disadvantages, the relative weights of which vary between different settings and intentions. The advantage of a closed group, such that attendees remain constant throughout the sessions (other than for reasons of non-attendance) is that it provides a more contained environment in which attendees may begin to feel more able to raise points that are of particular relevance to them, and thus gain the benefits of normalisation should other attendees validate their experience. Certainly by the time that topics such as 'thoughts and feelings' are addressed, there is a perceived advantage to attendees having the experiential knowledge that other people in the group may have similar experiences, and subjectively this is also the case when considering executive function, which comes closest to considering what some might term 'personality change' and can be perceived as very threatening to the integrity of self for individuals with brain injury. It is important to be clear that the materials contained in the following chapters have as their goal information provision regarding the cause, nature and management of common difficulties following brain injury, which is a rather different goal from being a classically therapeutic group. However, experience indicates that it is rare for some attendees not to divulge personal information, and so it is imperative that at the outset some ground rules are agreed with the attendees regarding confidentiality, and also making clear that there is no obligation to talk about personal experiences if people do not so wish. Once again, the advantages of having two facilitators include the flexibility that one can spend time individually with an attendee if this is appropriate, while the other continues with the group.

Open groups do not generate the same containment. Practically, too, although each session is suitable for use in its own right, if attendees wish to cover the whole range then they will need to attend all the sessions, or at least the bulk of them, and pragmatically this can be easiest to organise with a fixed list of expected attendees. Another common decision to be faced with is whether to run the groups separately for patients themselves, with another parallel group for carers/families, or whether to invite both patients and carers to the same group. Once again, there are advantages and disadvantages to both approaches. All parties attending the same sessions can be useful in fostering a joint approach to managing an externalised difficulty rather than the problem being identified with the person with the neurological condition, and can allay any fears of 'being talked about behind one's back'. Conversely, there are common and realistic difficulties associated with the role of carer that many carers would baulk at mentioning in the presence of their relative. However, thinking at the level of the family/carer system, there may be great utility in normalising and validating some of the difficulties that carers do face in the presence of all parties. Certainly, if one were to provide information to carers about, for example, behaviour changes after brain injury, then the onus would fall on needing to justify why this information should not be shared with the patient themselves rather than why it should be. The 'transparency' ethos espoused within cognitive behavioural principles can be a useful guide in such circumstances.

Numbers and attendance rates

The number of invitees to groups will depend on a range of factors, not least the physical facilities available, such as room space and chairs. While it is rather unproductive to be prescriptive about numbers, it is worth bearing in mind that there is likely to be some drop-out along the way; some of the literature regarding non-attendance rates include the somewhat demoralising figures that, while 75% of patients will attend an appointment that they themselves have arranged, this drops to 50% for an appointment that has been arranged for them (Sackett & Snow, 1979, cited in Myers & Abraham, 2005). However, this needs to be considered in the context of some of the literature presented in Chapter 1, in which the desire for information from patients and their families is a strong theme; for many individuals, the opportunity to attend sessions aimed at providing information is seen as a valuable opportunity.

This introduces the range of factors that can influence whether or not people will undertake to attend an intervention, and there is utility in considering the contributions of health psychology in attempting to structure health-related behaviours, as ongoing research may yet indicate that this has implications for recruitment to and attendance at rehabilitation interventions. While a number of models of health behaviour have been described over the years, one that has been applied in general rehabilitation settings in recent years is the Theory of Planned Behaviour (Ajzen, 1985). Wilson (2002) has described a multifactorial conceptualisation of the multiple models that can inform the process of neuro-rehabilitation, and the message from this is that there is much to be gained from considering models of behaviour that cross fields of academic research which have perhaps traditionally been separate.

The theory of planned behaviour (TPB) (Ajzen, 1985) suggests that people's behaviour is strongly influenced by their intentions, which in turn are influenced by three factors (attitude towards performing the behaviour, perceived subjective social norms, and perceived control). The TPB has been used to predict a range of health-related behaviours, such as attendance for breast screening (Rutter, 2000), testicular self-examination (Brubaker & Wickersham, 1990) and drug compliance (Hounsa, Godin, Alihonou & Valois, 1993). When used to structure information given to patients invited to attend a cardiac rehabilitation programme, the attendance rates increased to 86%, compared with a control group's attendance rate of 70% (Wyer, Earll, Joseph, Giles & Johnston, 2001). This most recent research suggested that similar interventions could optimise attendance at other programmes.

It was not until 2005, however, that the first study linking the theory of planned behaviour with engagement in neuro-rehabilitation was presented (Powell, 2005), concluding that just over half of the variance in intention to engage with rehabilitation could be predicted using a TPB-based scale. From this study, it transpired that the two factors that best predicted intention to engage with rehabilitation were the perceived advantages of attending rehabilitation and the perceived barriers to attendance. The potential to use such findings to maximise attendance rates is clear from the Wyer et al. (2001) study, in which structuring the appointment letter such that it reflected the TPB factors increased attendance rate by 16%. Work is currently underway to evaluate the effects of a similar theoretically-based appointment letter on attendance rates at a group intervention based on some of the material presented in this book, and it may be that moving away from atheoretical letters/posters relating to forthcoming sessions reaps benefits in terms of attendance rates.

One consideration related to patients' perceptions and attitudes towards rehabilitation – and hence subsequent engagement with it – relates to the recent emphasis in the NHS on Public and Patient Involvement, and in particular with the increasingly valued role of 'Expert Patients'. It behoves us as healthcare professionals to adopt a degree of humility when describing experiences that can be extremely threatening to an individual's sense of integrity of self (Blake, Burns & van den Broek, 2005); the benefits of normalisation that come from meeting other people undergoing similar difficulties to one's own may be transposed to the benefits of hearing someone who has been through a similar situation describing their own experiences in a sensitive and realistic manner, including both the positive and the negative aspects. When planning a course of sessions, it is well worth considering whether there is the option to invite a previous patient to speak for part of one session. Similarly, as healthcare professionals, we are obliged to take into account our own limitations in terms of skills and knowledge, and an initial transparent acknowledgement that we will be unable to answer every question regarding the huge breadth of relevant topics, from neuroanatomy to disability living allowance, can take some of the pressure of expectation off the facilitators. The advantage of running a series of sessions is that in the time between sessions it may be possible to find out information that can help to answer people's questions.

Material covered

The materials contained in this book are designed to have some inherent flexibility. Each of the sessions can be used in isolation if there is a need for a more focused single-session intervention, and there is some evidence for the utility of this approach. For example, evaluation of the materials in Chapter 5 indicated that at one-month follow-up attendees were using a mean of two additional memory strategies regularly (Champion et al., 2005). The chapters are, however, also intended to provide a logically ordered sequence of sessions, providing a basic introduction to the brain and brain injury, and then working progressively through a hierarchy of cognitive function and acknowledging the emotional implications of such difficulties. It is apparent that different settings and different populations will have different needs and priorities, and so sections that may be very pertinent in some circumstances may be better omitted under others. In order that sessions can stand alone as well as form part of a series, there is occasional repetition of information. This also reflects the overlap between some topics, such that, for example, some compensatory techniques are of relevance to both attentional and memory difficulties.

Chapter 8 contains three briefer considerations of common consequences of brain injury, and the hope with these is to increase the flexibility of the material such that one or more of these sections can be included alongside other, lengthier presentations as appropriate when planning the overall content of a series of sessions. The fact that these topics (language, dyspraxia and perception) are considered more briefly is in no way intended as an implication that they are any less important or have less of an impact on activities of daily living as some of the main sessions' foci. Rather, language is considered more briefly as one of the exclusion criteria for patients attending the sessions is likely to be dysphasia, and hence it is less likely to be relevant to group attendees, and for family/staff members the key message will be on enhancing communication skills, which is the focus of the language section of Chapter 8. Secondly, dyspraxia is considered rather more briefly because, despite the theoretical knowledge that allows for distinction between the different types of dyspraxia, in terms of practical management there is little to be gained from an exploration of this (Goldstein, 2004). Similarly, more detailed explanations of the theoretical underpinnings of perceptual disorders seem to add little to the general management advice that can be given within the confines of one session (Shaw, 2001), in contrast to the more detailed coverage of attention, memory and executive function. Further flexibility is provided by the brief information relating to 'frequently asked questions' in Chapter 9; for some groups, no attendees at all will be considering a return to work, while for other groups it may be of great relevance and so may form a more prominent feature of a session.

This introduces the balance of how much information to give, and the level at which to pitch it. The rule of thumb adopted in the following chapters is that sufficient 'theoretical' information is given in order to provide the rationale for some of the strategies that are subsequently suggested to manage difficulties. Referring once more to the theory of planned behaviour, the expectation is that individuals are more likely to act on the information they are given if they have a better understanding of why certain advice is being given, as this would relate to their perceived control of the situation and also the perceived advantages of applying a strategy.

It is clearly very easy to misjudge the depth of information to provide, as is reflected in the findings presented in Chapter 1 relating to the frequency of misconceptions and lack of understanding in the population of patients leaving hospital with a range of neurological conditions (e.g. Drummond et al., 1996). It would be naive to suggest that the same depth of information is appropriate across all settings, and between individuals within groups. With the overall goal in mind of explaining why the management strategies suggested can be helpful, the material in the coming chapters certainly simplifies neuropsychological models in order to make them more accessible and less overwhelming to people who are likely to be considering cognition for the first time. For example, in Chapter 4, a tripartite model of attention is presented (including sustained, selective, and divided attention). While this does have clinical validity (e.g. Robertson, Ward, Ridgeway & Nimmo-Smith, 1994), other commonly cited subdivisions of attention (e.g. orienting attention, focused attention, alternating attention) are not mentioned at all. This omission is intentional, and serves as a good example of the aim of this collection of resources. The material covered in the forthcoming chapters is by no means intended to represent a theoretical textbook of neuropsychology, as it would fall very far short of this ambition. Neither is there content in the coming chapters that is likely to come as new information to many healthcare professionals experienced in neuro-rehabilitation. It is also unlikely that everyone will view the content of the chapters as being close to any kind of 'gold standard' group session. The sole goal of this publication is to make it easier for the typically under-resourced healthcare professional to run an information provision group, by collating relevant information in one volume and providing ready-made resources; this publication is intended as a purely pragmatic therapy tool rather than an academic contribution to the literature. Obviously, individual professionals will have different views on how best to present information, but the intention of this material is to provide a basis that can then be tailored to individual requirements. For this reason, the material provided is likely to be over-inclusive for many settings, and once again this allows for flexibility of use of the materials. It is likely to be easier and quicker to omit slides and information than it is to add to them. Although the text within each chapter reads somewhat like a 'script', this is done for ease of use and to maximise the confidence of facilitators who may be less familiar with the topics being covered (should this be the case, it is important that at least one of the facilitators feels professionally competent to discuss matters of cognition, and it seems wise for a psychologist to be involved in facilitating the session on managing distress). The script is not intended as a gold standard appropriate for all occasions, and some information included may even be counterproductive in some circumstances. However closely to the content facilitators choose to adhere, one practical suggestion is for facilitators to familiarise themselves with the content in advance such that at no point will they have to read word for word from the script, an approach to presentation which does not aid the sustained attention of attendees. It is hoped that the slides provided will be of benefit to the facilitators in this regard, providing structure and cues to the relevant content.

When considering which sessions to run as a sequence of groups, it is important not only to consider the specific impairments of the attendees, should these be known, but also areas that the literature suggests are likely to become problematic in the future if they have not already. This particularly relates to the chapter on executive function. In practice, this session can sometimes feel somewhat awkward, and facilitators can feel that there is a danger of attributing blame to the individual with acquired brain injury or an ongoing neurological condition, by drawing attention to, for example, behavioural change. These elements are most closely linked to what some may call 'personality change', and their consideration can be extremely threatening to the integrity of the sense of self of individuals (Blake et al., 2005). The temptation can be to gloss over such topics in order to avoid any sense of confrontation. Sometimes this will be appropriate, in that with certain individuals a group setting will not be the best place to discuss such features. However, as with the other cognitive domains, there are advantages to be gained from the group setting itself. One very robust finding, however, which suggests that we should not shy away from mentioning changes in people's social interactions following brain injury (such as those relating to disinhibition, initiation or perseveration) comes from the literature relating to carer burden. Studies indicate that it is precisely these features that contribute most to the ongoing burden of caring for a relative with a chronic condition (e.g. Johnston & Maidment, 2004). While it may feel awkward to mention them, their acknowledgement can be very important for those providing informal care. Practically, this session (Chapter 6) tends to fit best later on in the sequence of sessions, partly because by this stage the relationships between the attendees may have developed such that people are less uncomfortable with potentially distressing information, partly because after a few sessions the hope is that some rapport will have developed between the facilitators and the attendees, and partly because by its nature executive dysfunction is a less tangible concept than, for example, memory or attention. The danger with presenting unfamiliar information that people may not be receptive to hearing early on in a course of sessions is that some attendees may not come back.

A number of references are included in the notes that accompany the slides in the following chapters. These are not intended to form part of the presentation in the group setting, as the source of the information is unlikely to be of primary relevance to patients and their families. They are included for the reference of the facilitator in order to acknowledge the source of the information and allow for further reading, should more detail be desired.

A compensatory approach to rehabilitation

It is important to acknowledge the theoretical approach adopted in selecting the rehabilitation suggestions included throughout the coming chapters. The approach adopted is entirely compensatory, with no inclusion at all of any restorative approaches. Not only does this have a sound basis in the 'functional adaptation' approach espoused by Luria

(1963), but more importantly it reflects the current state of the evidence base relating to clinically significant functional improvements in humans. Recent consideration of the current evidence regarding interventions aimed at the level of impairment rather than at the levels of activities or participation has led to this conclusion in the domains of memory, attention and executive function, among others (Evans, 2002b; Glisky, 2002; Park, 2002). While there is no complete consensus regarding the lack of utility of restorative approaches to lost function, and recent studies have brought the restorative approach back into the debate (e.g. Robertson & Murre, 1999), there remains little methodologically sound evidence at present suggesting that impairment level training has any clinical efficacy in humans beyond specific skill rehearsal.

Function is paramount when discussing cognition in relation to rehabilitation. Although it is useful to give the rationale for the presence of everyday difficulties, it is crucial to relate this explicitly to functional activities of daily living. Not only is this likely to aid comprehension of unfamiliar models of explanation, it will make the concepts being introduced more concrete, which is important when attendees may have difficulties with more abstract reasoning. While the material in the coming chapters includes common functional examples, wherever possible it can be useful to include examples relevant to the situations of attendees. If time permits, and if the attendees are willing to consider their own specific difficulties, there can be some benefit in considering potential management strategies as a group, drawing on the experiences of other attendees.

If running staff training sessions, it can be useful to try and make links with examples of patients with whom they will have worked (suitably anonymised). In practice, requests from staff for training often come at, or shortly after, a period when they are struggling to manage a particular patient, and so thought can be given in advance about how best to relate the information given to their situation while not polarising attitudes toward the patient further than may already be the case. Having described the reasons underlying, for example, a patient's challenging behaviour, it can be helpful to consider Ross's (1977) assertion that there is a tendency to misattribute actions to stable 'personality' characteristics of an individual rather than to temporary environmental stressors, and that this tendency can be exacerbated in hospital settings. Emphasising a focus on the behaviour rather than someone's disposition, and reminding staff of the importance of positively reinforcing desirable behaviours (and generating practical ways to do so) can help to keep the 'challenging behaviour' of an individual from being perceived as their centrally defining characteristic.

Involving other professionals

Having already acknowledged the potential benefits of involving an 'expert patient', there are also potential benefits to inviting other professionals to contribute to one of the sessions, depending on the needs of the attendees. Commonly, attendees have medical questions relating to their condition and associated topics such as medication, and if there is a medical professional available and willing to answer such questions in the group setting this can be a useful exercise.

Similarly, there can be advantages to inviting a social worker experienced with this client group to give information relating to, for example, the benefits available. This can serve as a direct source of information on a topic with which many health professionals feel ill-equipped to give information due to its perceived complexity, and the expert specialist knowledge of the social worker with experience in this field is an enormous asset.

Expertise relevant to returning to employment may be tapped into by contacting the Disability Employment Advisor from the local job centre, who may be able to advise on existing structures aimed at facilitating a return to work.

Depending on the attendees' needs, there may also be benefits to inviting local representatives of voluntary organisations that may be well placed to offer ongoing support, for example, Headway. Making such links can be an invaluable first step towards encouraging people to make use of such worthwhile and vital organisations.

Further practicalities

Practical arrangements to plan in advance include deciding at what time of day the group sessions will run. While circumstances will differ across settings, it is a common experience that family members or carers find it easier to attend at the start or the end of the day as they may well be having to continue to work. The desire to be accommodating of people's needs is a strong driver for many healthcare professionals, and facilitators may have the flexibility to run sessions in the early evening. However, there is a need to work responsibly and sustainably and this includes attempting to ensure that the boundaries of staff members are not eroded to the detriment of the service they are able to provide. If running training sessions for nursing staff, it is usually wise to discuss the timing with, for example, the ward manager, who will be able to advise on the times when most staff will be available (for example, just after handover).

Fundamental requirements for running a group session include the availability of a room that is accessible to wheelchairs, availability of sufficient chairs and the equipment required for the presentations (such as a laptop computer, a data projector and either a projection screen or an area of clear wall). The overheads and handouts are available on the website provided by the publisher (see box at the end of this chapter), and so access to the internet and printing facilities are necessary. A whiteboard and/or flipchart and pens are useful for several of the sessions, and, if available, an accurate model of the brain can be a useful visual aid. Some of the sessions described make use of other simple equipment and where this is the case it is specified at the start of the relevant chapter.

Inclusion of at least one break within each session is important, in order to reduce the effects of sustained attention difficulties. If the intention is to provide a drink during the break, then it is vital to check with the speech and language therapists concerned with any individual attendees that they are able to swallow safely.

Summary

Before running a group, planning is required regarding the practical arrangements such as the location, the equipment required and the timing of the sessions. Consideration must be given to the physical, cognitive and emotional presentations of potential attendees, such that they will be able to benefit from a group-based setting. Information given or sent to potential attendees can be constructed using theoretical models thought to be predictive of engagement with rehabilitation.

Supplementary web site

The slides and handouts included in this volume are available free online.
Visit www.wiley.com/go/neuropsych to access and download these flexible resources.

Chapter 3

Introduction to the Brain and Brain Injury

Comments about material

There is a balance to be struck in this session between giving sufficient knowledge and structure about brain function to underpin the explanations for functional difficulties that can arise after brain injury, hence providing the rationale for subsequent interventions, and giving an anatomy lecture. This first session has more of a focus on giving information than subsequent ones. An attempt is made to keep information grounded in functional examples, and the well-established finding that people with long-term neurological conditions commonly have a strong desire for information relating to their condition (see Chapter 1) means that attendees often have questions which can make the session more interactive.

Equipment required

In addition to the basic requirements described in Chapter 2, a model of the brain is particularly helpful for this session. If this is not available then a sketch on the flipchart or some other illustration can suffice. It can be informative to have a 3 lb/1.5 kg weight (which may be accessible from the physiotherapy gym) to give a concrete demonstration of the approximate weight of a typical brain.

Material to include

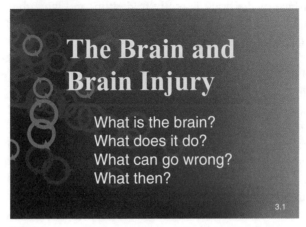

Slide 3.1

The plan is to start off by running through a few things that it's useful to know about the brain. The intention isn't to give a lecture about anatomy, but rather to give enough information to help make sense of some of the common consequences that arise when something occurs that affects how the brain works, whether that is a head injury, a stroke or some other medical condition that affects the brain. After we've thought a bit about what the brain is and what it does, we'll spend some time considering some of the common causes of disruption to the way that the brain works, and then the plan for the next few sessions is to focus on particular difficulties that can arise, such as memory or concentration, with a view to highlighting some practical suggestions to help manage them.

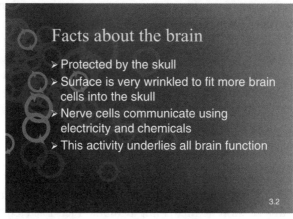

Slide 3.2

So, what do we know about the brain? [SHOW MODEL IF POSSIBLE, DIAGRAM IF NOT.] We know it's really complicated. It looks something like this, and it sits inside the skull, which provides some protection for it. The brain is about the size of a bag of sugar. We can see that the surface of the brain is really folded up, and what that means is that you can fit more brain into the limited space within the skull. It's a bit like crumpling up a sheet of paper; a flat sheet of A4 paper wouldn't fit into a little box, but it would if you crumpled it up. In fact, if you ironed out all the folds of the brain and laid it out flat, then it's been estimated that it would cover about the area of a broadsheet newspaper. Hence there's a lot of brain fitted into quite a tight space, and what we know is that there are billions of cells in the brain doing a wide range of jobs. About 1 in 10 of the cells in the brain are nerve cells called neurons, and it's these cells that are crucial in carrying out all the jobs that the brain does, whether that's moving your arm or remembering someone's name. The nerve cells send and receive signals using electricity and chemicals and it's this activity that underlies everything that the brain does. There are billions of nerve cells in the brain; a common estimate is 12 billion (Rose & Johnson, 1996) and there are very many more connections between all these nerve cells. There's a lot going on, and that makes sense when we think about what the brain actually does, because the answer to the question 'what does the brain do?' is basically 'everything'. A lot of what it does we never even think about in the normal course of events, and it's only when something goes wrong that it becomes apparent. For example, imagine you were to go to a football match and the team that you support scores a goal. What happens next? If we break down what a common reaction might be it might include:

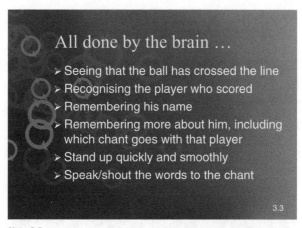

Slide 3.3

- Seeing that the ball has crossed the line.
- Recognising the player who scored.
- Remembering his name.
- Remembering more information about him, including which chant goes with that player.
- Standing up quickly and smoothly.
- Speaking/shouting the words to the particular football chant.

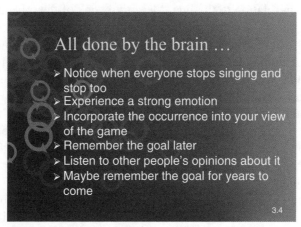

Slide 3.4

❏ Take into account when everyone else stops singing and modify your behaviour accordingly.
❏ Experience a strong emotion.
❏ Incorporate the new occurrence into your overall view of the game (are we now winning comfortably or do we need another goal to win?).
❏ Remember the goal later on when you are discussing the game.
❏ Listen to and understand other people's opinions on the goal.
❏ Maybe remember the goal and the associated emotions for years if it was a particularly notable/important one.

(After Powell, 1994)

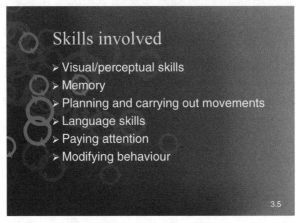

Slide 3.5

From that one example it's clear that there are many aspects to even the simplest of our experiences and activities, and the brain is responsible for all of them. Visual and perceptual skills are crucial; one of the brain's jobs is to make sense of information that comes in through your eyes, and make judgements about things like depth perception and where the ball was in relation to the line. Memory is one of the jobs that the brain does, and from that example we saw that recognising things or people and remembering things related to them has a very important effect on our subsequent behaviour and interactions with other people. Planning and carrying out movements is also down to the brain, as is finding the words that you want to say and actually speaking them. Language skills have a big impact on how we interact with other people. Paying attention and noticing social cues around you and fitting in with them (if you want to) so you don't act in a way that others would find strange are other functions of the brain. Feeling emotions and expressing (or indeed suppressing) them also relate to the brain's functions. Thinking flexibly, and altering your behaviour based on new information coming in, also involves the very front parts of the brain.

Normally we don't give all these skills a second thought, but if the brain isn't working as efficiently as it usually would, for whatever reason, there can be difficulties with any of the skills that we've just mentioned. The hope for the next few sessions is to provide some information about these skills in order to put some structure on the functions that the brain carries out, and so provide some explanation for the difficulties that might be relevant for you. The aim is then to cover some strategies that other people have found helpful in managing such difficulties.

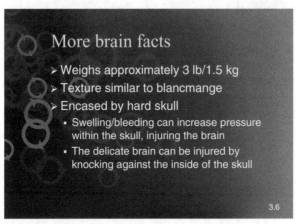

Slide 3.6

Here are some more facts about the brain. We mentioned that there's quite a lot of brain fitted into quite a small space, and it tends to weigh about 3 lb/1.5 kg [PASS WEIGHT ROUND]. It tends to weigh a bit more in men, but that really just reflects the overall difference in body weight (Rose & Johnson, 1996). Although it's heavier than many people might have imagined, it's actually fairly delicate. It's not as solid as a lump of muscle, but is often compared to the texture of a blancmange (Powell, 1994). That's why it needs protecting, and there are a number of ways in which it is protected. The most obvious is the skull, which provides a hard bony case around it [A SIMPLE DRAWING MAY BE USEFUL AT THIS POINT].

One implication of the skull being so hard and inflexible is that if there is any swelling of the brain, then there can be an increase in pressure within the skull, and that can lead to some damage. If there is any bleeding inside the skull, there'll be more pressure, and similarly if there is something like a tumour growing within the brain, that can cause difficulties as it will take up space and increase the pressure on the brain.

When something untoward happens, such as a head injury, the brain can bounce around inside the skull. Because the brain is delicate and the inside of the skull is very hard, the brain comes off worst and there can be damage to the brain. We know that certain parts of the inside surface of the skull are quite rough, particularly at the front behind the eyes. That's why after something like a car accident, there's often injury to the front parts of the brain just behind the forehead and at the front of these parts here [INDICATE FRONTAL POLES OF TEMPORAL LOBES]. We know that injury to these areas is particularly linked with difficulties in memory and planning, so we're already starting to see that the location of any injury to the brain is a big factor in determining what the day-to-day implications might be afterwards.

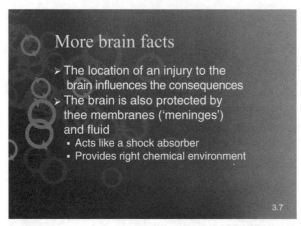

Slide 3.7

There's an extra layer of protection between the skull and the brain itself, which is a set of three membranes, a bit like three layers of skin. These are called the meninges, which is where we get the word 'meningitis', which refers to an infection involving these protective layers. This is why meningitis can be so serious and can have effects on how well the brain can carry out some of its tasks. Between the protective layers is a fluid that acts a bit like a shock-absorber, which protects the brain from knocks to the head, and it also gives the brain the right chemical environment to work at its best.

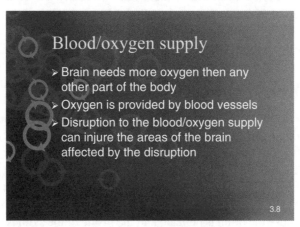

Slide 3.8

Just like all the other parts of the body, the brain needs oxygen to work, and just like every other part of the body, it receives that oxygen from the blood supply. Because the brain is so complicated it needs more oxygen than any other part of the body. Although the brain only makes up about 2% of the total body weight, it uses up 20% of the body's oxygen (Powell, 1994). The blood supply comes into the brain through a hole in the bottom of the skull, and then lots of tiny blood vessels go over the surface of the brain; some go deep into the substance of the brain, and others run in the space between the layers that protect the brain. Just like anywhere else in the body, the blood vessels bring along the oxygen that the nerve cells need to work properly, and they take away any of the waste products that are produced. If there is any disruption to the blood supply to the brain, then it can cause damage to the part of the brain which has lost its oxygen supply, and depending on which part of the brain it is, that can have a range of effects on day-to-day life. That is basically what happens in a stroke.

It has been mentioned several times now that it depends on which part of the brain has been affected as to what the consequences are. Although it's really a bit more complicated than this, for our purposes, it's helpful to assume that different parts of the brain do different things. We'll have a brief look at that before moving on to what can go wrong and what can be done about it.

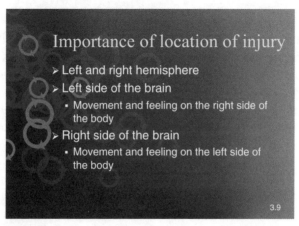

Slide 3.9

The first key factor to notice [MODEL OF BRAIN IS USEFUL] is that we can see that the brain is split into two halves, so you have a left-hand side and a right-hand side, and they're often called the left hemisphere and the right hemisphere. They are connected by a lot of nerve cells, but they usually do slightly different jobs. Already you can see that this is going to be very relevant, because it means that if only one side of the brain has been injured then we might expect all the jobs that the other side was more involved in to be less affected.

We know that the left-hand side of the brain plans and controls movement on the right-hand side of the body, and deals with feelings from the right side of the body, such as touch and pain, and awareness of where the limbs are in space. The right-hand side of the brain does the same for the left side of the body. For some reason, there's a crossover in these more physical tasks that the brain is responsible for, so if someone has weakness in just one side of their body, it's often the case that it's the other side of their brain that has been most affected.

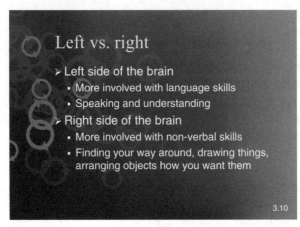

Slide 3.10

In terms of other jobs that aren't so physically obvious, it's usually the case that for most people the left side of the brain is more involved with language skills than the right side, so if there's an injury to the left side of the brain there can sometimes be difficulty with getting the words out that you want to, or with understanding what other people are saying, or with reading.

The right-hand side of the brain tends to be more involved with visual and spatial skills that are to do with non-verbal tasks, for example finding your way around a building, or drawing things accurately, or arranging things how you want them to be in relation to each other.

We could spend a long time going into lots of detail about the functions of various parts of the brain, but we're more concerned with getting towards practicalities, so we'll only have a very brief tour round the main areas of the brain. Common practice is to split the main part of the brain into four parts (often called lobes). Let's start at the back.

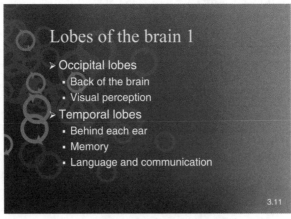

Slide 3.11

The occipital lobes are located at the very back of the brain [DEMONSTRATE ON MODEL OR PICTURE], and its main job is to do with visual perception. Information comes in through the eyes, and it runs along the nerve cells right to the back of the brain, where the occipital lobes make sense of the information, interpreting the information that comes in and starting to give it meaning.

Moving forwards, we've got the temporal lobe, which is a sausage-shaped part of the brain located just behind our ears. Remember, we've actually got two of each lobe, one on the left and one on the right, and that's going to be really important when we come on to thinking about ways to manage memory difficulties. The temporal lobes are very involved in various aspects of memory, for example recognising people and things, recalling information and making new memories. As we mentioned before, the very front parts of these temporal lobes are particularly susceptible to injury in an accident such as a car crash, which is why making new memories efficiently is one of the most common difficulties that people can experience after a head injury.

The temporal lobes also play a major part in language. Injury to the left temporal lobe in particular is associated with difficulties in either expressing yourself verbally or understanding what other people are saying verbally. The right temporal lobe is also involved with making sense of information that comes in through our ears, but has more to do with identifying noises in the environment rather than words (Temple, 1993), for example, appreciating the significance of approaching footsteps or a bicycle bell. If that is more difficult then it can be less obvious to other people than a difficulty with speech, but it can still have a marked impact on how we get through the day in a world where there's a lot going on around us.

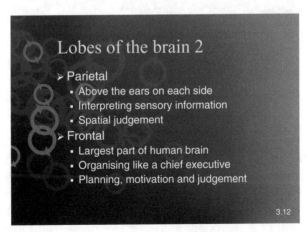

Slide 3.12

Just above the temporal lobe on each side of the brain is the parietal lobe. It can be hard to generalise what goes on here, but it clearly plays a part in the interpretation of information coming in through the senses and in interpreting spatial relationships between objects.

At the very front of the brain behind the forehead lie the frontal lobes. These are the biggest part of the brain in humans, and they carry out a whole range of functions that are important in our social interactions and in our ability to carry out tasks that crop up in day-to-day life. We'll be saying more about them in a later session, but it can be quite helpful to think of them as the manager of the rest of the brain, involved in planning the tasks that you want to do, making sure that things are running smoothly and making adjustments if necessary. The term that is often used for these sort of skills is 'executive function', which is a quite useful term because it makes you think of a chief executive of a company who would be involved in all those sort of planning and organising tasks and making judgements. Other aspects of frontal lobe function include motivation and initiation to start tasks, and also the ability to stop yourself doing something, so inhibiting behaviours. Once again, we saw that the frontal lobes are common sites of injury, and so some of these functions can become less efficient after an injury to the brain, which can have an impact on people's behaviour.

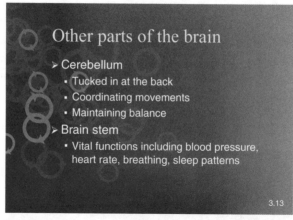

Slide 3.13

Just a couple more areas to highlight: there's a small cauliflower-like part of the brain tucked in underneath at the back. This is called the cerebellum and it is very involved in coordinating movements, which allows us to do things like ride a bike or change gear in the car, and maintaining balance. The brain joins up with the spinal cord, which is how messages get from the body to the brain and back again, and around the place where the spinal cord joins the brain, at the bottom of the skull, is what is called the brain stem. This is an area which controls all the vital basic functions, such as maintaining our blood pressure, our heart rate, our breathing, our sleep patterns and so on.

So that's a quick tour of the brain done. When we come onto specific difficulties we might mention the relevant areas in passing because it might help make sense of your own experiences, but from now on we'll be less concerned with anatomy and more concerned with the effects of injury or damage.

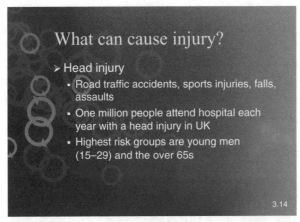

Slide 3.14

The term 'acquired brain injury' covers a range of causes, and tends to cover any process or experience that causes damage to the brain. There are a number of ways that this can happen and we'll run through these quickly.

One major cause is head injury, involving some sort of blow to, or sudden movement of, the head. Common causes include road traffic accidents, sports injuries, falls and assaults. One estimate is that every year one million people in Britain attend hospital having had a head injury (Powell, 1994). Men are more at risk than women, related to factors such as their participation in contact sports. It's young men in particular (aged 15–29) that are at most risk. The other high-risk group is the over 65s as they have more falls (Powell, 1994).

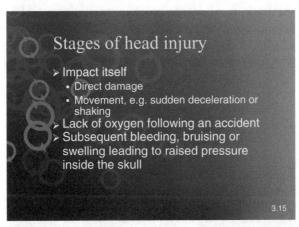

Slide 3.15

When a head injury occurs, a number of things happen that can injure the brain. Firstly, the impact itself can damage areas of the brain, either by going through the skull and damaging the brain directly or by nature of the movement that is involved, for example the sudden deceleration in a car crash. The delicate brain is shaken about and bounces against the inside of the hard skull. This movement can disrupt some of the communication pathways made up of connected nerve cells.

The second aspect causing injury is to do with a lack of the oxygen supply to the brain in the minutes after the accident. This is why first-aiders will always make sure that a person's airway is okay after an accident, because if oxygen isn't getting to the brain, it doesn't take more than a couple of minutes for some of the nerve cells to die.

Thirdly, in the hours and days after the brain injury there can be more bleeding, bruising or swelling of the brain, which can cause damage as it causes the pressure inside the skull to increase and press on the brain.

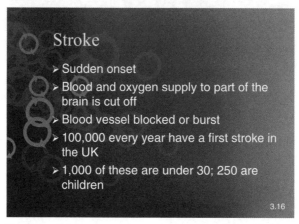

Slide 3.16

There are other causes of brain injury. A stroke is another very sudden cause, in which the oxygen supply to a part of the brain is cut off, either because the blood vessel supplying that part of the brain has become blocked, or because a blood vessel has burst, often due to a combination of a weak blood vessel wall and high blood pressure. There are about 100,000 people in this country who have a first stroke every year. Although often thought of as something that only affects older people, over 1,000 of these are aged under 30, and 250 every year are children.

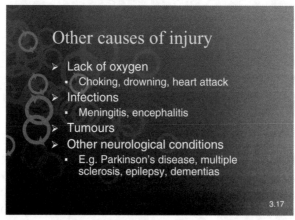

Slide 3.17

A lack of oxygen getting through to the brain can occur when something happens like choking, or drowning, or after a heart attack. If there have been a few minutes where the brain hasn't been getting enough oxygen then there is a strong likelihood that some of the nerve cells will have died and so the brain will have been injured.

Infections can happen in the brain: meningitis and encephalitis are perhaps the two best known ones. If there is a neurological condition such as a brain tumour, then this too can have effects on how the brain functions, as it is taking up space within the skull and therefore putting pressure on the brain.

In addition there are a range of neurological conditions that commonly have an impact on the functioning of the brain. These include conditions such as dementia of one sort or another, and a range of others including Parkinson's disease, epilepsy and multiple sclerosis. Their symptoms are often due to the effects of the neurological condition on the substance of the brain or the electrical or chemical communication within it.

We can see that there is a range of things that can cause some sort of injury to the brain, by various processes. We've seen that the brain controls many skills that we take for granted, and so after some sort of injury to the brain we commonly do see difficulties arising with some of these skills. Although the cause of the difficulties can be quite different, some of the consequences can be similar – for example, memory difficulties – because the key factor is that there has been some involvement of the brain, which has made certain skills less efficient.

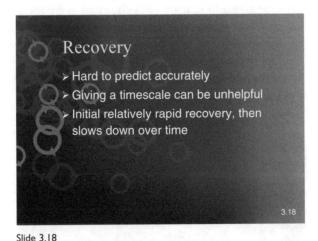

Slide 3.18

For many, if not all, people, the key questions are 'what can be done about it?' and 'what can be expected in terms of improvement and recovery?' One thing to acknowledge first of all is that it is pretty much impossible to predict with accuracy the extent and the timescale of recovery. Some people will make estimations like 'six months' or 'two years' but these are of questionable value (Meacham, 2005).

One pattern we do commonly see after an injury to the brain of the sort that is more of a 'one-off' incident rather than an ongoing condition, is for there to be initially fairly rapid improvement in the difficulties that resulted (although it may not feel very rapid at the time for the individual and their family), and then a gradual slowing of improvement, as shown by this graph.

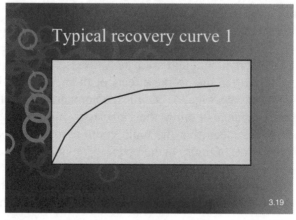

Slide 3.19

There deliberately isn't a timescale on this, as that varies enormously between individuals, and often it's only when you look back over the time since the injury occurred that you start to be able to gauge how much improvement is still going on at a given point. What you can see is that at some point, improvement generally becomes very slow indeed or effectively stops. It can be the case for many people that the recovery stops short of the previous level of ability for particular skills, for example concentrating on an activity for an extended period of time.

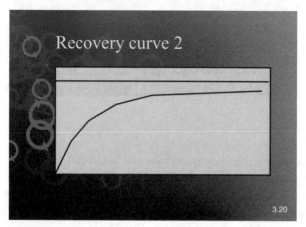

Slide 3.20

The approach that is most helpful in practice is to find ways to reduce the impact of any shortfall on day-to-day life, by putting into place strategies to manage the difficulties. That can either involve changing the demands that face you or using compensatory strategies to help you play to your strengths. It's this area that we'll be focusing on particularly in the coming sessions. The emphasis is very much on management rather than cure, because that's the approach that has been shown to be most effective. Adopting that approach also gives us more cause for optimism, because even though any improvement in how well the brain can carry out a certain task may have slowed almost to a stop, it's often the case that people and their families are still able to become better skilled at managing the ongoing difficulties, and as such reduce some of the limitations on daily life that may have arisen.

Even though this graph isn't so relevant for people who have a neurological condition that didn't have a sudden identifiable onset, that theme of getting better at managing the difficulties rather than trying to mend them is just as relevant.

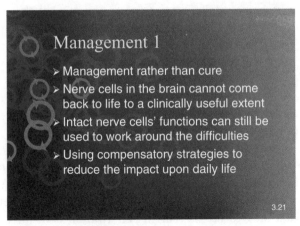

Slide 3.21

We know that when a nerve cell in the brain dies for any of the reasons that we've mentioned, it can't come back to life, and that is the bottom line that often limits the usefulness of trying to work on restoring the skills of the brain. We've already mentioned that different parts of the brain specialise in different skills; that's a very useful consideration for us in trying to manage ongoing difficulties, because even though there may have been some cells that died in a part of the brain due to the injury, there's plenty of other cells that are still intact and carrying out their functions perfectly well. Sometimes we can use these intact skills to work around the difficulties that arise, and in doing so we can lessen the impact of any shortfall from previous levels of ability.

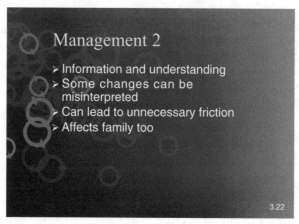

Slide 3.22

In trying to do that it seems vital for everyone to know what the difficulties are; the first step in trying to work around a problem is to identify it and understand it. One intention for these sessions is to provide sufficient information to understand the nature of any ongoing difficulties well enough to try and find ways to reduce their impact.

It can also be very useful to have a better understanding of the reasons for some of the changes that can occur when the brain is injured in any way because some of the changes can have effects on the way that people interact with the people around them, and these can be open to misinterpretation. For example if it's more difficult for someone to listen to someone else speak for more than a few minutes because the skill of concentration isn't working so efficiently at present, then that can easily be misinterpreted by someone who isn't aware of the difficulties as being a bit rude and not interested in what they're saying. Having an awareness of the reasons underlying any changes in behaviour can be very useful in reducing any unnecessary friction in families.

Having mentioned families, it's often said that any condition affecting the brain doesn't just affect an individual person, but rather it affects the whole family. Involving family members and loved ones can be a vital part of becoming aware of the nature of any difficulties and then having a joint approach within the family to manage them in a negotiated way that doesn't feel like nagging. There is of course a lot of distress associated with the conditions we'll be thinking about, and for many people and their loved ones this can be summed up with a theme of 'losses', be that a loss of some independence, or a loss of some future plans, or a loss of the roles that different people fulfil. That is as relevant for family members as it is for the individual who has one of these conditions, and one of the sessions will focus more on the emotional side of managing ongoing difficulties and the realistic distress that that entails.

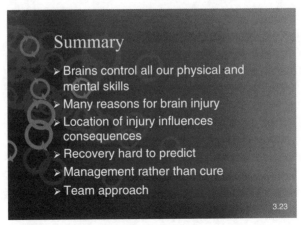

Slide 3.23

In summary, we've seen that the brain is a very complicated organ of the body that controls all of our activities, including the mental skills that we normally take for granted. Different parts of the brain are more involved in certain skills than others so the location of any injury to the brain is very relevant to any subsequent difficulties. It can be useful to think about these difficulties as being inefficiencies of specific skills rather than making any sweeping conclusions about being less intelligent, which very often is certainly not the case. There are a whole range of reasons for the brain being injured, including sudden events like a head injury or a stroke and more enduring neurological conditions.

Recovery can be very hard to predict but a useful approach is to try and reduce the daily impact of any persisting difficulties by using compensatory strategies rather than trying to build up the skills again like some sort of mental muscle. We also acknowledged that the sort of difficulties we've been thinking about frequently cause distress both for the individual concerned and their loved ones, and one hope is that the coming sessions will provide enough information and practical suggestions to enable all concerned to be more aware of the nature of the difficulties and have a little more sense of control over them.

Introduction to the Brain and Brain Injury

The brain has a wrinkled surface in order to fit in as much brain into the limited space within the skull as possible. It contains billions of cells; about one in ten are nerve cells ('neurons'), which communicate using chemicals and electricity. It's this communication that underlies every function of the brain, and subsequently every single activity we carry out.

This includes a vast range of skills, including visual and perceptual skills, remembering things, planning and organising, language and communication skills, and the ability to concentrate, as well as carrying out movements and essential tasks such as keeping our heart beating.

The brain is delicate and so is protected by the skull, and by three membranes within the skull. It is surrounded by fluid that contains the right balance of chemicals for the brain to function at its best.

While the fact that the skull is hard is usually very useful in protecting the delicate brain, when things go wrong it can have some disadvantages. For example, a blow to the head may cause the delicate brain to bounce off the inside of the hard skull causing some injury. Because the skull is hard, if there is any swelling or bleeding inside the skull, then the pressure inside it can increase and cause injury to the brain in that way. Similarly, if there is something else taking up space within the skull, such as a tumour, then that too will increase the pressure.

Although it's a complex picture, it can be helpful to think of different parts of the brain as being more involved with certain types of tasks. This is useful to know when considering how to manage the effects of any injury to the brain. The left side of the brain and the right side of the brain are often involved with different skills. The left side of the brain controls movement and feeling on the right side of the body, while the right side of the brain controls movement and feeling on the left side of the body. In addition, the left side of the brain tends to be involved with verbal and language skills, while the right side of the brain is more involved with visual and spatial skills.

Causes of brain injury

- Head injury – including road traffic accidents, sports injuries, falls and assaults.
- Stroke – oxygen supply to part of the brain is cut off, usually due to a burst blood vessel or a blocked blood vessel. Stokes can affect young people and children as well as older people.
- Lack of oxygen to the brain – choking, drowning, heart attack.
- Infections – e.g. meningitis, encephalitis.
- Other neurological conditions – e.g. brain tumours, epilepsy, Parkinson's disease, multiple sclerosis.

Recovery and management

It is hard to predict the timescale and extent of recovery after an injury to the brain. After, for example, a head injury or a stroke, there is often relatively rapid recovery at first, which then slows down. If there are persisting difficulties, the most useful approach is 'management rather than cure', i.e. finding ways to work around the difficulties. As different parts of the brain are more involved in different skills than others, then this means that there are often lots of remaining strengths to play to that will help in managing any difficulties.

Chapter 4
Attention

Comments about material

A tripartite model of auditory attention is described in this session, consisting of sustained, selective and divided attention, in addition to visual attention. Clearly this does not cover the various other elements that have been described clinically and in the literature, such as orienting attention and alternating attention. It is hoped that this simplification strikes a balance between accuracy and accessibility of information to people who may be unfamiliar with concepts of cognition. There is some clinical justification for choosing these three hierarchical levels of attention (e.g. Robertson et al., 1994). Although there is a lack of consistency in the literature in terms of nomenclature, the three levels described here feature by some name in all common models (e.g. Levitt & Johnstone, 2001). In combination, they sit well with Parasuraman's (1998) conceptualisation of the range of functions commonly grouped under the banner of 'attention', which are essential in 'allowing for and maintaining goal-directed behaviour in the face of multiple, competing distractions' (Parasuraman, 1998, p.16).

The task used to demonstrate the difference between sustained and selective attention is of course strongly linked with auditory working memory, but serves the purpose of demonstrating the limits on information processing and the interference effects of distractions.

Equipment required

In addition to the basic requirements described in Chapter 2, some mechanism of providing an auditory distraction is needed, be that some loud music to play or some way of making a loud sustainable noise.

Material to include

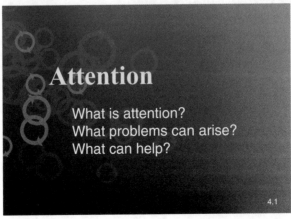

Slide 4.1

One common difficulty that arises for people who have had a brain injury or have a neurological condition of some sort is a difficulty with attention or concentration. In fact, there are
different aspects of attention that the brain is involved with, and it's not uncommon to have
difficulties with one or more aspects of attention but to have no problems with other aspects.
The plan for this session is to consider what we mean by attention, then to look at what can
go wrong after the brain is injured in some way, and then based on that we'll come on to
some suggestions about how to reduce the impact of these difficulties on everyday life.

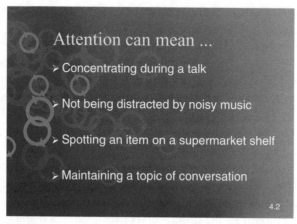

Slide 4.2

It's tempting to assume that 'attention' is a single thing, as if we are simply good or bad at
concentrating. In fact though, attention can relate to a range of things, for example maintaining your concentration while listening to a talk, being able to concentrate on what
you're doing without being distracted by noisy background music, spotting what you're
looking for on a supermarket shelf, or staying on track with the topic of a conversation.

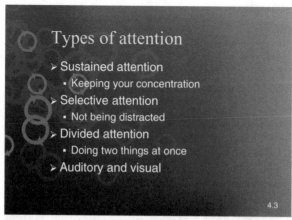

Slide 4.3

To make sense of these different things which we refer to as 'attention', a helpful way to think about it is to split it into three levels of increasing difficulty. The most basic level of attention is the skill of maintaining your concentration on something, which is usually called 'sustained attention'. A bit harder than that is the task of keeping your concentration when there are other things distracting you, which is called 'selective attention'. The hardest task of all is often called 'divided attention', which relates to a situation in which someone is trying to do two or more things at once. After an injury to the brain there can be difficulties at any one of these levels, so we'll have a look at each one of these in turn.

It's also worth remembering that although we often just think about concentrating in terms of listening effectively to spoken words, it also has a large part to play in efficiently scanning what we see in front of us and finding things we're looking for. Problems with attention can be both auditory and visual. There are strong links between paying attention to things we hear and things we see, which is why ventriloquism works. If we hear something and see something at the same time, our attention systems link them together (Spence & Driver, 2000).

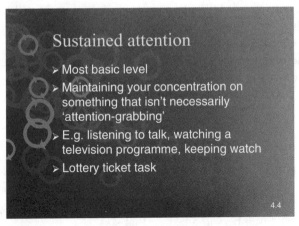

Slide 4.4

The most basic level of attention that we'll be considering is sustained attention. This is what most of you will be doing as you listen to this, that is maintaining your concentration on something ongoing that isn't exciting or unexpected enough in itself to give you a shock and grab your attention in the way that a loud noise would. Another example would be watching a television programme; if you're watching *Coronation Street* then you need to maintain your attention for half an hour to follow what's going on. Another example closely linked with sustained attention would be keeping watch, in the way a sailor would on a warship. This skill is particularly difficult, because for most of the time there might be nothing happening at all, but they have to sustain their attention for when something does occur.

That's an extreme example in which someone may have to stay focused for several hours, but we all have a limited ability to maintain our attention – most of us have probably experienced how hard it is to keep focused during a very long film or play or lecture. After an injury to the brain, that limit can be reduced, so that it can be even harder to stay focused, and concentration can wander after a much shorter time, sometimes seconds. This can make it very hard to follow a brief conversation, let alone a half-hour television programme.

If it's harder to keep your attention on, for example, a conversation, then the likelihood is that you'll miss some of the information that the other person is saying. Thinking briefly about memory, we know that the first part of making a memory is getting the information into the brain in the first place. If you've missed out a detail because your mind was wandering, then it doesn't matter how good your memory is at storing information or retrieving it when you want it, you won't be able to remember it because it was never paid attention to so it never 'went in' in the first place. It's common in people who at first appear to have memory difficulties for at least some of the difficulty to be due to attention difficulties. Some of the memory strategies that work quite well for many people are aimed at the first part of memory, that is, getting the information in and paying attention to it.

We'll try a task now, and it will serve two purposes. Firstly it'll make the point that there is a limit to how much information we can attend to at any one time, and secondly it'll help us start to think about the next hardest level of attention.

I'm going to read out the numbers from a national lottery ticket, so there'll be six numbers. Have a listen to them and then try and write them down or just say them in your head. [READ THE NUMBERS OUT SLOWLY:]

9   26   15   31   22   17

How did you get on? That uses a skill that is sometimes linked with maintaining your attention, but also involves your ability to keep information in mind temporarily. It's probably the case that not everyone managed to get all six, because most people can recall between five and seven numbers in a task of that sort.

Let's try that task again; I'll read out the numbers on a different lottery ticket, you listen to them and then try and recall them again. This time we'll have something going on in the background as well though. [PLAY SOME MUSIC LOUDLY OR MAKE A SUSTAINABLE DISTRACTING NOISE BY SOME OTHER MEANS.]

18   44   6   39   12   32

How was that? There's every chance that it was rather harder than the first time round, and of course that's what you'd expect because we had something noisy distracting us. That introduces us to the second level of attention, which is harder than straightforward sustained attention. This often gets called selective attention.

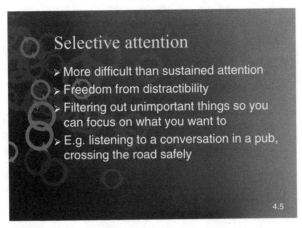

Slide 4.5

Selective attention involves staying focused on a task without being distracted by other things that are going on. For example, if you're able to concentrate on what I'm saying even when there are noises outside such as sirens going past, you're using selective attention to filter out the things that aren't immediately important so that you can focus on the things that are important. Everyday examples would include having a conversation in a busy, noisy place like a pub, where you need to filter out everyone else's conversations, the music on the jukebox and the flashing lights on the fruit machines, so that you can focus on what the person next to you is saying. Being able to watch *Coronation Street*, even while there's loud music coming from next door, would be another example. When we do things in real life, we often do them in situations where there are lots of other things going on to distract us. If you think about something like crossing the road safely, there are any number of noises and visual distractions that need to be filtered out so that you can concentrate effectively on making sure that you won't get run over.

As we saw when trying to concentrate with the distracting noise, selective attention can be difficult for anyone at the best of times. If the brain has been injured in some way, it can become even more difficult, and it can become impossible to stop yourself being distracted by things that are going on around you, or things that you're experiencing such as pain, headaches, or even things that you are thinking to yourself. The difficulties with selective attention can be very marked even if sustained attention is pretty good, and it can have a marked impact on interaction with other people in real-life settings where distractions are common, for example trying to work out change in a shop which has background music playing. There can also be potentially serious safety risks; if someone is cooking sausages under the grill and the doorbell goes, then they can be distracted from the task in hand, not go back to the sausages and a fire can start.

The third and final level of attention we'll think about is called divided attention.

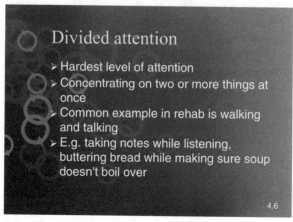

Slide 4.6

This is the hardest level of attention, and basically involves trying to concentrate on two or more things at once, for example watching *Coronation Street* while doing the ironing. This is something that everyone finds harder than either sustained attention or selective attention. We made the point earlier that for all of us there is a limit on our resources for attention, and even if we're able to keep focused on one task despite distractions, it can be hard for our brains to allocate the resources that we have between simultaneous tasks so that we don't mess up one of the tasks. If it's hard at the best of times, you can imagine that this skill is particularly vulnerable when there is an injury to the brain, and difficulties with dividing attention are very common after a brain injury.

One example that is seen in a hospital rehabilitation setting when someone has difficulties like this is for the person who's had the brain injury to be practising walking with the physiotherapist, and it's going pretty well but taking a lot of effort and concentration for them to make the movements and keep their balance. If someone walks past them and says 'hello', and the person stops and tries to have a conversation with them, then they can be at risk of losing their balance and falling over, because they can't concentrate on the conversation and standing up at the same time.

One thing that people who experience this kind of difficulty often say they find difficult is being part of a group of people who are all talking at once, for example at a family gathering or when there's a lot of visitors to the hospital bedside. It can feel very overwhelming and it's not uncommon for people to have to leave the situation (if they are able to) because it feels that there is too much going on for them to cope with.

As with the distractibility, there are safety concerns with this level of attention too. If you're heating some soup and at the same time you're buttering the bread to go with it, then there is the danger that, because it's hard to keep two things in mind at once, the soup will boil over.

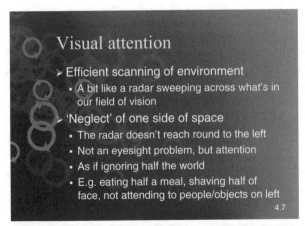

Slide 4.7

A lot of our examples have been to do with conversations and paying attention to the information that comes in through our ears. It's also worth thinking about what can become more difficult with paying attention to information that comes in through our eyes. We can call this 'visual attention'. In the normal course of events we scan the environment around us, a bit like a radar which sweeps across what's in our field of vision, picking up the details. In a similar way to how we pay attention to people's speech, we can then focus on what is important to us, ignoring things that are irrelevant. Sometimes we can 'keep our eye on' more than one thing at once, for example if we're looking for something in a shop and at the same time making sure that our children aren't up to mischief. Just as details of a conversation can be missed when someone has difficulties with attention, visual details from the scene in view can be missed too, and the scanning of the environment can become less efficient.

This can lead to difficulties with everyday tasks. For example, finding something on a supermarket shelf takes quite a bit of efficient scanning in order to search through all the other items and find the one thing that you're looking for. It can be easier to be distracted by some other things and pick those up instead, and it can all feel rather overwhelming too as there is so much competing for attention.

In social interactions with other people, there are quite a lot of very subtle social cues that people use naturally and we normally pick up on without really thinking about it, like glancing at your watch to indicate that you need to finish the conversation, or raising your eyebrow to indicate that you're joking (van Zomeren & Brouwer, 1994, cited in Levitt & Johnstone, 2001). If it's harder to pick up subtle visual details because of a visual attention difficulty, then this can have an impact on the quality of social interactions.

There's one particular consequence of an injury to the brain that is worth mentioning because, as well as having particular safety implications, it highlights the fact that this difficulty with scanning isn't a problem with eyesight itself, but with paying attention to what the eyes are able to see. It's called 'neglect', not meaning neglect in the way that it's most commonly used, but meaning that people seem to neglect to pay attention to one side of space, usually the left. Using the analogy of the radar, it's as if the radar stops its sweep before it gets to the left-hand side of space, so that it seems as if the person is ignoring that side of the world (Halligan & Marshall, 1993). It can seem very strange, and is often mistaken for an eyesight problem, but is more to do with visual attention, although it can happen alongside difficulties with vision. Common consequences include people leaving food on the left-hand side of their plate, sometimes only shaving half of their face, or seeming to ignore people or objects on their left-hand side. It's as if 'half the world has suddenly ceased to exist' for them (Mesulam, 1985). That kind of inefficiency in visual scanning has a big impact on day-to-day life – just think about crossing the road, for example – but even when the effects aren't so marked, inefficient scanning of what's around you can have an impact on your daily activities.

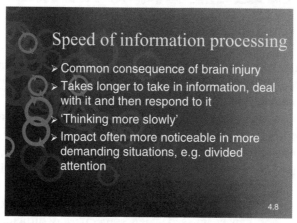

Slide 4.8

Although it's maybe not immediately obviously linked with attention or concentration, it seemed sensible to mention at this point something else that people often experience after an injury to the brain. People often feel as if they're 'slowed down', and that, although they're still very able to work things out and respond accurately to questions and situations, it just takes them longer.

This is very common after any sort of injury to the brain, and is to do with the speed at which the brain can deal with information. If the speed at which the brain can process information is slowed down, it may take longer to take in information in the first place, longer to deal with it and work out how to answer or react, and then longer to actually carry out the response. By the time those three stages have taken a bit longer, there can sometimes be a noticeable slowing in people's interactions; they can remain as accurate as ever, but there can be a delay in replying, and the subjective experience is of 'thinking more slowly', or 'thinking through mud'. This can be particularly noticeable in situations that are more demanding, for example when trying to do two things at once, or if there are a lot of distractions, or it's a particularly abstract or complicated task you're having to respond to.

One reason why difficulties with information processing often come up when thinking about difficulties with attention is that the speed at which information is presented can have a big impact on how easy it is to take in that information. When I was reading out the lottery numbers earlier, I did it fairly slowly so you had time to take them in, but if I'd read them out quickly one after the other it would have been much more difficult. If you think about how we talk with people we know well, we often speak very quickly and jump from one topic to the next without a moment's pause. If, because of a brain injury, it's taking someone longer to deal with incoming information then they're going to miss a lot of what is said if it's presented too fast for them to deal with. That can look like an attention difficulty, and subsequently a memory difficulty, when in fact it may be at least partly due to a slowing of the speed at which information can be processed.

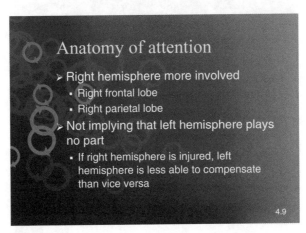

Slide 4.9

We've covered the main areas of attention that we're going to, so we'll quickly consider the link with brain injury, run through some common implications (some of which we've already mentioned as we've gone along), and then come on to some of the most common suggestions for reducing their impact on day-to-day life.

There are various parts of the brain that are involved with attention – bits at the front are thought to be involved with intentionally allocating resources, bits at the back are thought to be more involved with less deliberate management of attention. The right-hand side of the brain tends to be more involved with managing the various systems of attention than the left-hand side, particularly the frontal part behind your forehead and the parietal part, just on the side of your head (e.g. Pardo, Fox & Raichle, 1991).

That's not to imply that the left-hand side of the brain isn't involved in attentional skills, as it does play an important part, but the right-hand side is particularly good at it – if the left-hand side of the brain is injured, the right-hand side can often keep things running along pretty well in terms of attention, but if it's the right side that's injured, then the left side can't quite keep things going, which is the reason why that neglect of one side of space more frequently affects the left-hand side than the right.

After something like a head injury in a road traffic accident, it's very common for the front parts of the brain to be affected due to the sudden deceleration causing the front of the brain to bounce against the hard inside of the skull. We just mentioned that the front parts of the brain are involved with allocating the limited attentional resources available to us, and that's why it's common for people who have had this sort of head injury to have particular difficulty with divided attention tasks.

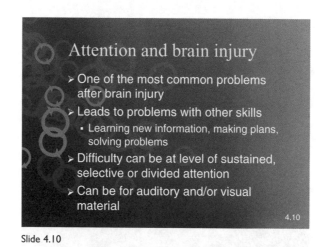

Slide 4.10

Difficulty with attention is one of the most common consequences after an injury to the brain caused by a head injury or a stroke. Because it is such a fundamental skill, it has knock-on effects for other skills such as memory, making plans or solving complicated problems, because to do many of these things you need to be able to concentrate for long enough to carry out the task. We ran through the three basic levels of attention, and it can be the case that the difficulty can lie at any one of these levels; sustained and selective attention could be intact but divided attention could be a problem, for example. However, if sustained attention was more difficult, then it's most likely that the two harder levels would be even more difficult. We also mentioned that attentional difficulties can affect information that comes in through our ears but also information that comes in through our eyes, so both auditory and visual attention can be affected.

We've mentioned a few examples of how attentional difficulties can affect day-to-day interactions, but here are a couple of slides with the kind of things that people often notice that can be attributed to difficulties with attention:

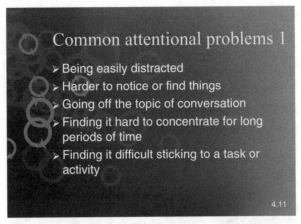

Slide 4.11

Examples include being easily distracted from the task in hand; that can include going off the topic of conversation when something occurs to you or catches your eye. It can be hard to find or notice things if there are lots of other distractions in front of you. Even without distractions it can be harder to stay concentrating on a particular task for long, for example reading or following the plot of a television programme. Sometimes it can be harder to stick at a task when it's more effortful to concentrate.

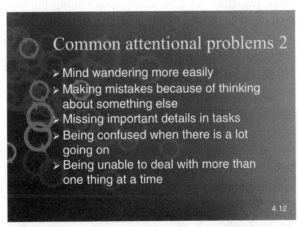

Slide 4.12

People commonly say their mind wanders more easily, and if that's the case when you're doing a particular job, that can lead to making mistakes because your mind is elsewhere. Important details can be missed either in conversations or in the activity that you're involved in.

Difficulties can arise in more complex situations when there's a lot going on. It can feel overwhelming and confusing in busy places with lots of people talking at once, or in a work setting with many demands on you. It can be particularly hard to carry out accurately more than one task at once.

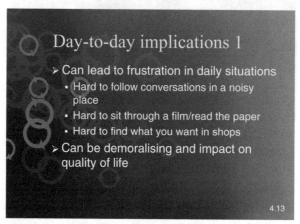

Slide 4.13

It is clear that it can be very frustrating for someone who is experiencing these kinds of difficulties, and they can have a big impact on quality of life. It can be harder to obtain pleasure from previously enjoyable activities, such as talking to friends in a pub, or going to the cinema to watch a two-hour film, or sitting and reading the paper for half an hour. Daily tasks such as shopping can take much longer, and it can feel very demoralising to be made aware that it's harder to rely on your ability to concentrate than it might have been in the past. Sometimes people start avoiding situations that they know will be difficult for them, and may run the risk of becoming socially isolated and starting to become depressed.

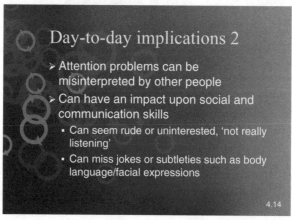

Slide 4.14

As well as being frustrating for the person who has difficulties with attention, by their very nature, concentration difficulties can be misinterpreted by other people. People who don't know that it's harder for the brain to keep its focus on the task in hand might wrongly assume that the person is being rude and not showing interest in what they're saying. As we mentioned before, it can be harder to pick up on non-verbal cues, such as body language and facial expression, so social skills can be affected; for example, it might be harder for someone who has difficulty with visual attention to pick up the cues that the person they're talking to is yawning or looking at their watch, which would normally be our cue to stop talking.

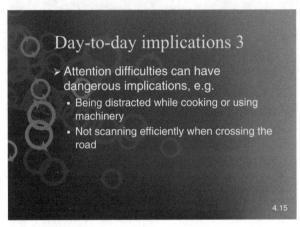

Slide 4.15

We mentioned earlier that difficulties with attention caused by an injury to the brain can have safety implications, and that is an important point to emphasise. It's not being overly dramatic to say that being distracted while cooking or using machinery can have fatal consequences, as can crossing the road when you're not able to scan the road effectively or quickly enough to be aware of all the traffic.

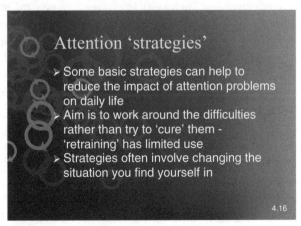

Slide 4.16

The key question is 'what can be done about it?' Although there are no magic answers, there are some basic strategies that can help to reduce the impact of attention problems on daily life. The most effective way to reduce their impact is to try and work around the difficulties rather than try to 'cure' them (e.g. Park, 2002). In practice, the most effective approaches often involve changing the environment around you to reduce the demands on your attention; the approach is very much 'management' rather than 'cure'.

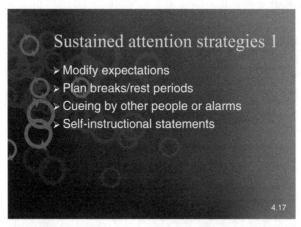

Slide 4.17

First of all, it's important for the person with the brain injury and the people around them to be aware of what aspects of attention are difficult for them, so that's why it's important for us to have covered what we have so far. The first couple of points on this slide should follow on directly from that – if you know that concentrating for long periods is more difficult for you at the moment, then change your expectations of what you want to achieve or how long you plan to spend achieving it. Although that can seem like 'failing' somehow, and it can be painful having to acknowledge that something is more difficult than it used to be, making a reasonable adjustment to your demands on yourself is usually preferable to continuing to set yourself unrealistic targets, and then continually not quite meeting them and becoming more and more demoralised. A good starting point is to allow extra time. If you usually spend 20 minutes reading the paper, allow yourself 40, or say you'll only read the sports pages, showbiz gossip and the headline story in your usual time (or whatever is most important to you). In addition, within that time period, make yourself take breaks where you will have a rest. If you know from experience that after 10 minutes your attention starts to wander and so you waste a couple of minutes, plan to have a 2-minute break after 8 minutes (using a kitchen timer can help with this) in which you do something else like make a drink or do some relaxation exercises, so that you don't lose any extra time and can start afresh for another 8-minute burst of activity.

If you do find that your attention wanders off-task, that in itself can make it hard to implement strategies to manage your attention without the help of someone or something else to keep you on track. Other people can be invaluable here in bringing you back on track. It needs to be someone you feel comfortable with giving you a prompt or a cue, because pointing out that you've gone off the topic is a personal thing to say, and from certain people it might be very unwelcome. If you are going to ask someone to help in this way, it can be helpful to decide in advance what words they'll use (maybe something like 'how are you getting on with what you're doing?'), otherwise it may quickly start to feel like they're just nagging, which isn't nice for either person.

It may even be that you don't need another person, but an alarm clock or kitchen timer set to go off at intervals may serve the same purpose of cueing back to the task in hand (Robertson, Mattingley, Rorden & Driver, 1998). Writing a self-prompting statement of your own choice on a sticker on the alarm can mean that you receive the prompt to re-focus without having to rely on someone else, maybe something like 're-focus – what am I trying to achieve?' If you do become aware that your attention is wandering in between times, it can be worth having a similar set phrase that you say to re-focus yourself.

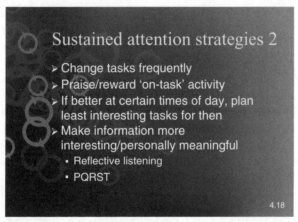

Slide 4.18

Planning ahead can make a difference. Changing tasks frequently can mean that you don't lose track of the task in hand before you stop doing it, but a bit of planning is required to make sure that you get through the whole of a task in the day if you want to. If you estimate one task will take you an hour, allow some extra time so as not to put pressure on yourself, and split it into several chunks, which you can then alternate with other tasks, making sure you can fit in all the chunks during the day.

It can be encouraging to have an incentive for tasks achieved, so allowing yourself 'rewards', such as 'I'll have a cup of tea when I've done 20 minutes work on this', can keep you going. For friends and relatives, praise and encouragement for time spent 'on task' is important, rather than negative comments about the times when distractions do happen.

More individualised planning can be helpful; if you are affected by a long-term neurological condition, there's every chance that you and your family will become experts on your particular difficulties and how they affect you throughout the day. You'll know if there are particular times of day at which you find it easier to concentrate, and if there are particular places where you find it easier to concentrate. If that is the case, then plan to carry out the least interesting jobs you have to do at those times, as it'll give you the best chance of doing at least some of them.

Common sense and personal experience tell us that we all find it easier to concentrate on something that we find interesting and is personally meaningful to us. There are techniques to try and make information that you are hearing or reading more interesting, and more personally meaningful, which in turn makes it easier to concentrate and take the information in. Two of these strategies are ones that are covered when we talk about memory strategies, but we will briefly mention them here as well.

Firstly, reflective listening involves trying to paraphrase what someone has just said to you, picking out the main gist of it – for example if a friend says 'I'm going to France for a fortnight with my sister and her husband' you could say something like 'so you're off to the continent with the family – are you looking forward to it?'. This gives the advantage of extra processing of the information, as you've had to extract the important parts from it, and done in moderation is usually perceived as showing interest in what the person is saying.

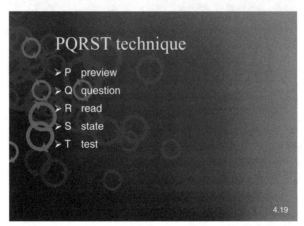

Slide 4.19

Secondly, the PQRST technique also increases the extent to which information is processed by the brain, but is used for written material, such as that in a newspaper article. The 'R' in PQRST stands for 'read', so before you even read the article that you want to concentrate on there's the 'P' and the 'Q' to get through. The 'P' stands for 'preview' and what you do here is just work out the gist of what the story's about, which in a newspaper you can usually do from the headline. The 'Q' is a key element, and it stands for 'question'; from the gist of the story, ask yourself what you'd like to know by the time you've read it. If you were to see someone later in the day and they asked you about it, what would you hope to remember about it? Then you read the article, and then you read it again, which is the 'S' standing for 'stating' it back to yourself and trying to link it back to your own questions. Finally 'T' is for 'test'; can you now answer your questions about the article? Of course this is too time-consuming to do for everything you read (and papers won't always report all the information you'd be interested in), but for important things it can be a very effective way of giving written information structure and personalising it to your own interests, which helps with concentration and subsequent memory.

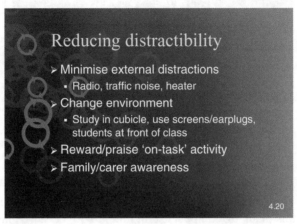

Slide 4.20

The key element in managing difficulties with selective attention is to try and reduce the likelihood of being distracted. Some of the most successful approaches involve making changes to your immediate situation where possible. The most obvious, but most crucial, step to take is to try and eliminate anything that could distract you while you want to be able to concentrate. This can mean turning the radio off when you're trying to read or cook, or moving to a different room if you can hear noisy traffic going past or if there's a noisy heater in the room. At work it can mean finding a quiet area to work in, which might take some negotiation with your employers. In more academic settings, studying or reading in a cubicle at a library can reduce distractions from things going on around you, and some people find using earplugs helpful. In a classroom or lecture setting, sitting at the front is worth trying as there'll be fewer people between you and what you want to focus on. In hospital rehabilitation settings, it's often helpful for the physiotherapists or occupational therapists to put portable screens around people when they're practising something in the gym so that they can concentrate and not be distracted by other people in the gym.

As we mentioned earlier, rewarding yourself and giving yourself incentives is a good approach. A knowledge of why things are harder now and why you are having to make adaptations is important for you and your family. That's especially the case because there will always be some situations – particularly outside the home environment – where it is not possible to remove all the distractions, and so it is important for you and your loved ones to have realistic expectations about what you'll be able to manage.

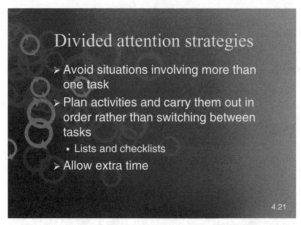

Slide 4.21

When it comes to divided attention, planning in advance is very important. Involving someone else with this planning can be a useful thing to do, because making a complicated plan can involve divided attention skills itself, so by its very nature may be difficult to do without some extra help.

If you know that a situation is going to be problematic because there will be more than one thing competing for your attention at once, then, if possible, you want to find a way to avoid it being like that (Levitt & Johnstone, 2001). That applies to situations in which there will be multiple things coming at you (e.g. listening on a phone while checking something on a computer screen) and also situations in which there are multiple responses you need to make (e.g. speaking while typing).

Structuring the task so that you can achieve the goal you want to while doing only one thing at a time is the key point. For example, you would make a note of what the telephone instructions were, hang up, then find the information on the computer screen, and then ring back with the answer. It will take longer but if divided attention tasks are more difficult then, as we mentioned above, it is helpful to modify your expectations as to how much will be achieved and how quickly. Even though it takes longer, the task is more likely to be accomplished accurately.

When trying to impose a 'one at a time' structure onto complicated tasks, using lists and checklists can prove very useful. Having things written down and organised so that you can refer to them means that there's one less thing for you to have to carry in your mind, as otherwise you'd also have to concentrate on where you were up to in the overall plan. Having things established as a routine is something that can be effective too (Levitt & Johnstone, 2001), because once a sequence of events is so familiar that it requires less conscious effort to carry it out, then it is less demanding on our limited attentional resources. The message is very much to plan ahead and try and establish routines in which you never have to do more than one thing at any one time.

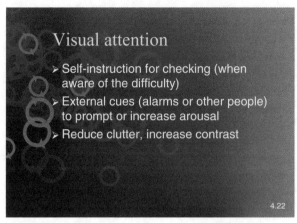

Visual attention

> Self-instruction for checking (when aware of the difficulty)
> External cues (alarms or other people) to prompt or increase arousal
> Reduce clutter, increase contrast

4.22

Slide 4.22

If someone is aware that they have a difficulty with inefficient visual scanning, then they can sometimes cue themselves to have several looks at the scene ahead of them, and check that they haven't missed what they are looking for. Sometimes, somebody else is needed with them to give them that prompt to check that they haven't missed anything.

In the case of neglect, it's often very difficult for people to be aware of the fact that they are missing out on something. By definition, attention isn't being paid to things on that side of space, so it can be hard to recognise that there's anything missing. That means that there can be a difficulty in knowing that there is a difficulty at all, and that means that people can put themselves in dangerous situations like trying to drive or cross roads when it really isn't safe. In these circumstances, it's usually safest for people to be accompanied when outdoors for their safety and that of other people, because then the people with them can act as the prompt or cue to draw the person's attention towards something.

Aside from either cueing yourself to scan extra carefully or being cued in by somebody else, two other general principles are helpful in situations where you have more control over the environment, such as in your workspace. Firstly, reducing clutter means that there are fewer visual distractions when you are trying to find something, and fewer items competing for your attention. Secondly, increasing the contrast between colours of objects against their backgrounds can be helpful in making them easier to find. For example, if the brake on a wheelchair is hard to locate, it is often a useful idea to wrap some brightly coloured tape around it so that it stands out more. This can be applied to many items that can routinely cause frustration if they are hard to find, such as keys.

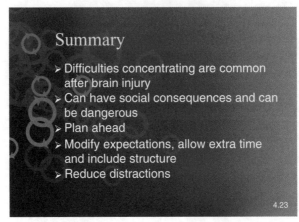

Slide 4.23

In summary then, we've seen that difficulties with attention are very common after an injury to the brain. There can be a difficulty with maintaining concentration, or being distractible, or having trouble dealing with more than one thing at once. This can have an impact on daily tasks and on social interactions with people, and can be quite dangerous in certain circumstances.

Making changes to the situations in which you will need to concentrate is the first step. Reducing distractions, allowing extra time and structuring the activity to include planned breaks are good basic strategies. It may be helpful to enlist someone else to help planning and structuring the tasks that you want to carry out, bearing in mind some of the information that we've covered in this session.

Attention

Difficulties with attention or concentration are very common after any injury to the brain, whatever its cause. There are different sorts of attention, and it may be that one or more aspects become less efficient while others remain intact. Attention can be thought of in terms of three levels of increasing difficulty:

1. Sustained attention – the ability to keep your focus on the task in hand, for example when reading a book or watching a television programme.
2. Selective attention – the ability to filter out distractions, for example being able to read a book even when other people in the room are talking.
3. Divided attention – the ability to concentrate on two or more things at once.

Attention is also necessary to take in visual information efficiently, for example scanning the supermarket shelves to find an item. This also becomes more difficult when there are distractions and you have to 'keep your eye on' something else as well. Sometimes it is harder to pay attention to one side than the other.

Examples of difficulties with attention can include going off the topic of conversation, having difficulty finding things, finding it hard to stick to a task for an extended period of time, or missing important details. These difficulties can be particularly apparent in busy, complex situations such as at work or in social settings.

As well as being frustrating and having an impact on social and work settings, difficulties with attention can have marked safety implications. Road safety, cooking and using machinery all require efficient concentration.

Another common difficulty related to taking in information effectively is to do with the speed with which the brain can deal with information. Sometimes after an injury to the brain it takes longer to make sense of information coming in, and longer to plan and carry out a response. Although the accuracy may be just as good as ever, the fact that it takes longer can have an impact on daily life; for example, if someone is speaking quickly then it may be harder to take in all the details of what they are saying.

Managing attention difficulties

The most successful approach to reducing the impact of difficulties with attention on daily life is through 'management' rather than 'cure'.

Sustained attention

1. Modify your own and other people's expectations. Allow extra time to carry out a task, and plan breaks within it.

2. Arrange a 'prompt' to refocus you on the task in hand. This can either be another person saying a phrase that you are happy with, or an alarm set to go off after a little while.
3. Plan ahead. Plan the day so that what you want to achieve is split up into manageable chunks, taking into account the times of day that you find it easiest/hardest to concentrate.
4. Try and make information you need to concentrate on more interesting; summarise the main points and think about how they might relate to you.

Selective attention

1. Reduce distractions; turn off the television/radio, take work to a quiet room.
2. Modify your own and other people's expectations in settings where distractions cannot be eliminated.

Divided attention

1. Plan activities such that only one task needs to be carried out at once. This may take longer but is likely to be more accurate. When imposing a 'one at a time' structure to the day ahead, using lists and checklists can be helpful.
2. Establish routines that don't involve carrying out more than one task at once.

Visual attention

1. If practical, prompt yourself to double-check.
2. Reduce clutter to eliminate visual distractions.
3. Increase the contrast in colours between objects and their background (e.g. coloured key fobs).

Chapter 5

Memory

Comments about material

The description of the various different aspects of memory is clearly not exhaustive, with no mention being made, for example, of sensory memory. As is the case for the other chapters, this represents an attempted balance between accuracy and accessibility of information, and serves to make the point that memory is not a unitary function. Some of the examples used to demonstrate the selective nature of brain injury may not be appropriate for all groups. For example, where the effects of alcohol on memory processes are used as an example, this may be sensible to omit if the group members include those with substance misuse difficulties.

Equipment required

In addition to the basic requirements described in Chapter 2, a model of the brain can be useful, as can a newspaper article to demonstrate the PQRST technique. A newspaper can also be a source of non-famous faces for rehearsing face/name association.

Material to include

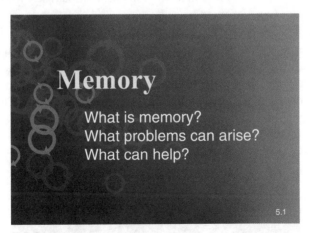

Slide 5.1

Difficulty with remembering things is one of the most common difficulties that people experience after a brain injury (Evans, 2003). The main aim of this session is to consider some strategies that people have found helpful in reducing the impact of memory difficulties on their day-to-day lives, and in order to do that we'll firstly consider what memory is and what can go wrong.

Often people will say 'I have a terrible memory', as if memory is just one thing that is either 'good' or 'bad', but in fact memory is many different things (Parkin, 1999).

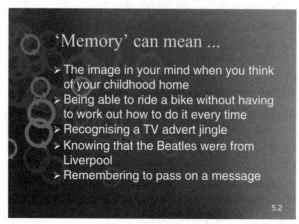

Slide 5.2

'Memory' would include the image that comes to mind when thinking about your child-hood home. It would include skills that you've learned such as riding a bike or playing the piano, that you don't have work out how to do afresh each time. It would include knowing what an advert on the television is for when you hear the familiar piece of music playing. It includes knowledge of facts that you have learned, such as knowing that the Beatles came from Liverpool, and it also includes remembering to do things in the future such as pass on a message. It's clear that 'memory' encompasses a whole range of skills, and there are different types of memory.

An injury to the brain can affect certain types of memory while leaving other types of memory intact. It's important to know which types of memory might still be strengths for us, because then we can play to those strengths and try to use them to compensate for the types of memory that may have become less efficient. We can try and put some structure onto the different elements that come under the broad heading of 'memory'.

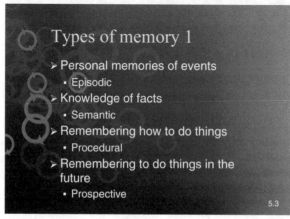

Slide 5.3

There's no need to worry about knowing the technical names for the different types of memory, but they can give a useful framework to the different aspects of memory. Firstly, we remember things that have happened to us, like birthdays, holidays or meetings; as that involves remembering particular episodes in your life, that is often called 'episodic' memory.

Knowledge of facts, like 'the Beatles came from Liverpool' is a separate aspect of memory called 'semantic' memory, and would be called on if you were taking part in a quiz or being asked a question at college or work. Skills such as riding a bike, driving a car or playing the guitar all rely on learned procedures that have been rehearsed over time, and so remembering how to do these things is called 'procedural' memory. A common experience for all of us, even without any injury to the brain, is forgetting to do something that we were meant to do. That relies on 'prospective' memory, memory for a future event.

It is important to acknowledge that all these aspects of memory can be affected to different degrees by a brain injury. For example, procedural memory is fairly robust and resistant to injury. If someone is trying to learn how to do something new after a head injury that has made their episodic memory (memory for events) weak, they may end up in the situation that they know how to carry out the new skill but don't remember having learned how to do it. For example, on a hospital ward, if someone walks from their bed to the physiotherapy gym every day for several weeks, then it might be that they're then able to remember how to get there (as their procedural memory is intact) but are unable to remember having been there on previous occasions (because of their impaired episodic memory). Although it can begin to become complicated, the key message from these subdivisions is that although a condition affecting the brain can make some aspects of memory less efficient, it may be the case that other aspects of memory remain strong and can be used to work around some of the difficulties.

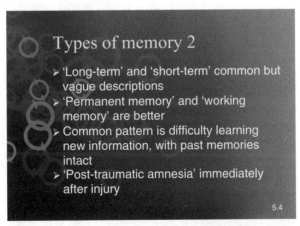

Types of memory 2

> 'Long-term' and 'short-term' common but vague descriptions
> 'Permanent memory' and 'working memory' are better
> Common pattern is difficulty learning new information, with past memories intact
> 'Post-traumatic amnesia' immediately after injury

5.4

Slide 5.4

One of the most common things that people say after a head injury is that 'my long-term memory is good but my short-term memory is bad'. That introduces us to another distinction between different types of memory. In fact, it's not very helpful to describe memories as 'long' or 'short' term; after all, how long is 'long' and how short is 'short'? Two much better terms are 'permanent memory' and 'working memory'.

Working memory is a temporary memory store in which we keep information in mind while we need it. The classic example is remembering a telephone number by repeating it under your breath while you dial it. That is what has often been called 'short-term memory', and it's clear that it covers a matter of a few seconds rather than hours or days. Estimates vary, but some authors suggest that this sort of temporary working memory can store approximately two or three seconds' worth of information (Aggleton, 1997).

This can be demonstrated by trying to remember sequences of random numbers, e.g. 3729546. Most people can remember between five and seven numbers like this, and no more than that, because that's how many numbers fit into this short, time-limited temporary memory store. Interestingly, that explains some of the differences you see when you ask people who speak different languages to do a task like that. For example, Welsh-speaking people have been shown to find that particular number-repetition task harder than English-speaking people; they can repeat fewer digits, because the words that represent each number take longer to say than their English equivalents (e.g. one is 'pedwar', two is 'chwech'), and so fewer of them can fit into the limited time-span of the working memory store (Aggleton, 1997).

If that's what we mean by working memory, then permanent memory is anything that is remembered beyond a few seconds. For example, remembering what you had for breakfast would be permanent rather than working memory, and so would be just as 'long-term' as what happened a year ago.

What people tend to mean when they say they have difficulties with 'short-term memory' but not with 'long-term memory', is that they can remember things from before they had their brain injury, but have more difficulty remembering things that have happened since then, including what they did yesterday or what they had for breakfast this morning. That is the most common pattern of memory difficulties after a brain injury, and words like 'long-term' and 'short-term' aren't necessarily the most helpful way to describe it. This is a good way to look at it:

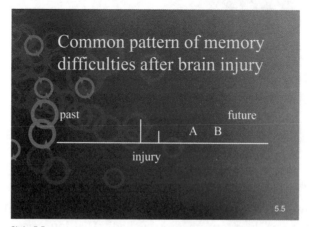

Slide 5.5

Memories made before the injury or the onset of neurological difficulties are often intact. This means that people can remember their last birthday or holiday before things became more difficult, but the difficulty lies with learning new information after the injury. Something that happens at point A [ON SLIDE] can be hard to remember accurately by point B. After a sudden onset injury such as a head injury, there is often a period of time just before and just after the injury for which people aren't able to remember what happened. The length of time for which people have no memory before the injury sometimes decreases with time, but often people are left with some 'blank' time. After a head injury, there can be a period of time immediately after the injury occurs where it is very hard for people to form any new memories at all, and this can be very confusing, disorienting and distressing. This can last anything from hours to weeks or more, and is called 'post-traumatic amnesia'.

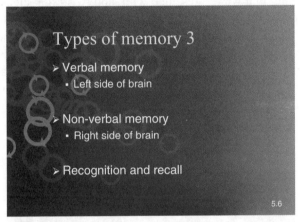

Slide 5.6

One very important distinction to make is that, broadly speaking, the left-hand side of the brain and the right-hand side of the brain deal with different sorts of information [USE MODEL OF BRAIN IF AVAILABLE TO DEMONSTRATE THE TWO HEMISPHERES]. In most right-handed people, the left hemisphere is more concerned with language skills, while the right hemisphere is more concerned with visual and spatial skills. This pattern is true of memory skills just as much as any other skills. The left side of the brain plays a bigger part in remembering verbal information, for example remembering someone's name or an address, while the right side of the brain plays more of a part in remembering non-verbal information, for example faces and directions. For example, if you remember any of what has been said in this session later today, that will involve the left side of your brain, but if you remember what the people here look like, that will involve the right side of your brain. What this distinction means is that if someone has an injury to one side of their brain only, then they might have difficulties with only one of either verbal or non-verbal memory, with the other remaining intact. That's one of the key things that a good assessment of memory will look for; often people will have difficulties with, for example, non-verbal memory but will be able to use their intact verbal memory to try and work round some of the problems it raises.

One last distinction to make is between recognition memory and free recall of information. This can be a particularly important distinction for family members and people close to someone who is having memory difficulties to appreciate.

If I were to ask you to draw the face of a 20 pence piece (after Aggleton, 1997), you'd probably be shocked to see how difficult you found it. Although you might feel sure that it has the Queen's head on one side, you may be less sure which way she's facing, or which words or symbols are present, or even how many sides it has. Most people find this hard to do accurately. If, however, I were to show you a selection of three or four different coins, and ask you to pick out which one of the coins is the 20 p piece, it would be really very easy for most people. This example demonstrates how much easier it is for us to recognise something that we're presented with, and so all the 'clues' are there in front of us, than it is to recall information with no clues there to help us. That's the difference between 'recognition memory' and 'free recall' of information, in which you have to retrieve information with no clues to help you. In practice, this means that just because someone with memory difficulties recognises somebody when they see them, does not mean that we should assume that they can remember other information about them, such as their name, their job or what they talked about last time that they met. The fact that recognition is easier than recall can mask a lot of difficulties.

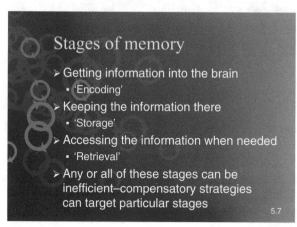

Slide 5.7

Three are three basic stages involved in making a new memory. Firstly we need to get the information into the brain, which is called 'encoding'. Secondly we need to keep it there, which is called 'storage', and thirdly we need to be able to access it when we need it, which is called 'retrieval'. In the context of a brain injury or neurological condition, any or all of these stages can be affected. Once again, this is where a good assessment can be helpful because it may indicate at which stage it would be most useful to aim compensatory strategies.

These three stages can be affected to different degrees. For example, alcohol has its effects mostly on the encoding stage. If you imagine someone going to the pub and getting drunk, then it may be that they have trouble remembering what happened the next morning, because the alcohol they drank made it harder to form new memories by interfering with their encoding. If they'd been doing a pub quiz while they'd been drinking, it may be that they actually did pretty well at it, because the alcohol wasn't interfering so much with their ability to retrieve the information that they needed to answer the quiz questions (Aggleton, 1997).

There are a number of factors that affect the first, 'encoding' stage of memory formation. Information doesn't just enter our heads in the same way for everyone; without even thinking about it we put our own personal structure on incoming information. For example, imagine an art critic walking around an art gallery (Aggleton, 1997). He'd be looking at the paintings and the exhibits, seeing who the artists were, making judgements about their quality and how well they were displayed. Now imagine an art thief walking through the same art gallery. He'd be noticing totally different things, such as where the skylights are, and where the alarm systems and cameras are. Exactly the same information would be available to both of them, but they would come away with very different memories of the art gallery because of the different personal structure that they imposed on it.

Our ability to organise information can have an impact on how well we encode new information, and also on how efficient we are at retrieving it when we want to access it. The ability to organise information is a separate skill that can be affected by brain injury. This highlights the fact that, very often, people with memory difficulties don't have a memory difficulty in isolation, but can also have difficulties with planning and organising. If someone has difficulty concentrating, then that will have an impact on encoding, because if you're not able to concentrate well, then information won't 'go in' as well. If that's the case, then even if the 'storage' and 'retrieval' stages aren't affected, people may seem not to remember things that they've been told. Sometimes what can initially seem to be a memory difficulty is better explained in terms of being a concentration difficulty.

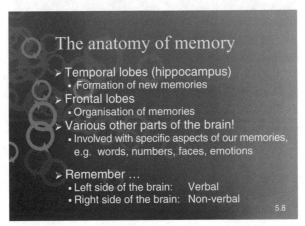

Slide 5.8

The effects of brain injury often depend on which parts of the brain have been injured. Quite a lot of the brain has some part to play in maintaining efficient memory skills

[USE MODEL BRAIN IF AVAILABLE]. The parts of the brain most commonly linked with memory are the temporal lobes, which are sausage-shaped parts of the brain located on the side of the head just above each ear. One particular part of each temporal lobe called the 'hippocampus' is particularly linked with the formation of new memories (Evans, 2003), and has been much studied. In itself, it's quite memorable because it is shaped a bit like a seahorse, and the name 'hippocampus' comes from the Greek for 'seahorse'.

The frontal lobes of the brain, located just behind the forehead, are very involved in organising and planning. Because of that, they are relevant for encoding new information and accessing it when required. In addition, many other parts of the brain are involved, depending on what it is that's being remembered. Different areas are more particularly involved with words, numbers, face recognition or particularly emotional memories.

A key point to make again is that the different sides of the brain tend to deal with different types of memory, so damage to the left hippocampus would have more of an impact on verbal memory, while damage to the right hippocampus would have more of an impact on non-verbal memory.

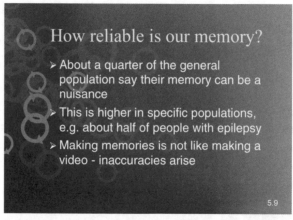

How reliable is our memory?

➤ About a quarter of the general population say their memory can be a nuisance

➤ This is higher in specific populations, e.g. about half of people with epilepsy

➤ Making memories is not like making a video - inaccuracies arise

5.9

Slide 5.9

How reliable is our memory under normal circumstances? The quick answer can seem to be 'not very'! About a quarter of the general population (not people with any injury to their brain at all) report having difficulties relating to memory to the extent that it's a nuisance (Thompson & Corcoran, 1992). That's about one in four people, and that is a figure that is important to acknowledge. When people are experiencing memory difficulties it can feel very embarrassing and stigmatising for them. Knowing that it's something that a lot of people have some degree of trouble with on a daily basis, albeit to a lesser extent, can be a helpful piece of information to keep in mind. There will be some one-off situations, such as going into a shop and not being able to remember what you came in for, that can make people think to themselves 'the other people here must think I'm stupid'. If that is going through your mind then you may feel very self-conscious indeed. Bringing to mind the figure that one in four of the general population might have a memory lapse at some point in the day can take off some of the pressure that you might be putting on yourself. Of course it's distressing when you're having difficulties time after time, but in some situations other people won't know how often you struggle, and might be putting it down to 'just one of those things' that affect 25% of the people they meet in the day, rather than jumping to any negative conclusions.

The figure does, as you might expect, increase in groups of people who do have some neurological involvement. For example, about half of people with epilepsy report significant memory problems (Thompson & Corcoran, 1992).

Making memories isn't as accurate as making a video recording of something. It's been suggested that there are two sources of information that go into our recollection of an event. Firstly there's information that arises from our experience at the actual time of the event, and secondly there's information that arises from your own (or other people's) subsequent explanations or assumptions about what happened (Loftus, 1979). After some time has passed, it can be very hard for us to distinguish between the two sources of information and we can be convinced that we remember something happening when it might not actually have happened quite the way we remember it.

A large proportion of the general population report difficulties with remembering things. Everyone has forgotten something at some point in their life; everyone knows what it feels like to forget something. What do you think are the three most common difficulties with memory that people report? [ATTENDEES GENERATE IDEAS.]

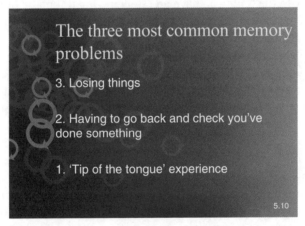

The three most common memory problems

3. Losing things

2. Having to go back and check you've done something

1. 'Tip of the tongue' experience

5.10

Slide 5.10

The third most common memory difficulty that people report experiencing is losing something, for example putting something down and not remembering where you put it. At number two is something that everyone will have done at some point in their lives, which is having to go back and check you've done something, such as turning the oven off or locking the door. The most commonly reported memory difficulty is not being able to find the word you want, but having the feeling that it's 'on the tip of your tongue'. While this can represent a difficulty with the language areas of the brain, it can be viewed as a classic 'retrieval' problem (Aggleton, 1997). The word is clearly 'stored' in the brain because very often we can be aware of what letter the word starts with, or whether it's a short word or a long word, and we can describe what the word means. As soon as someone says the word, we recognise that that was the word we were searching for.

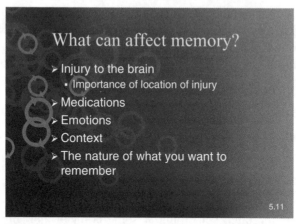

Slide 5.11

Various things can affect how efficiently the various aspects of our memory work. Clearly some form of injury to the brain can have an effect, be it a traumatic brain injury, a stroke or a progressive neurological disease. The location of the injury within the brain has a large influence on the sort of difficulties that may result. For example, damage to the left hemisphere is likely to cause more difficulties with remembering verbal information. Damage to the frontal lobes (which play a large part in the organisation of memories) may mean that although the content of memories are formed fairly accurately, the context is incorrectly remembered. For example, someone may remember the details of something that they were told, but not who told them it or when (Moscovitch, 1992).

Many medications are known to have side effects and these can include effects on memory. Some of the common types of medication that can affect memory are drugs to control epilepsy, as well as some drugs used to help with psychiatric conditions. Some of their effects on memory can be explained by a more general effect on alertness and speed. Never stop taking any medication without discussing it with your doctor first.

Our emotions can have an impact on how well we remember things. If someone is extremely frightened or anxious it can make remembering things more difficult. It's been well demonstrated that if people are depressed, then the 'encoding' stage of their memory is not so effective, and so new information is not processed as deeply as it could be. It's also been shown that when people are depressed, they have more of a tendency to bring to mind negative memories that fit in with their mood state, and it's much harder to bring to mind positive memories (Cropley, Macleod & Tata, 2000).

That introduces the idea of 'context'. An often-quoted experiment involved people who were training to be divers and whose assessment was a task carried out underwater. The study showed that those divers who had practised the task underwater, where they would actually have to do it, did better than those who had revised on dry land (Martin & Aggleton, 1993). That relates to the external context of the environment around you, while depressed people's retrieval of memories is affected by their internal context, that is, how they are feeling.

The effects of alcohol can serve as another example of 'internal context'. Normally, if you're asked to remember something but something else distracting happens before you have to recall it, that interference can make your recall less efficient. However, one study showed that if you were sober when you're asked to do the remembering, but the interference task happens while you're drunk, the interference has less of a negative impact on subsequent performance because it happened in a different internal context (Aggleton, 1997).

Obviously, what it is that you're trying to remember has an impact on how well you remember it. After watching the news, it may be that you are able to remember more about the sports news than the financial news. If you watch an international football match, it's likely that afterwards you'll be able to remember more of the names of your own country's team than those of the opposition. We all remember information better if it is more interesting to us, more familiar and more meaningful.

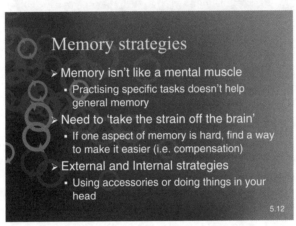

Slide 5.12

If there are difficulties with some aspects of memory, then there are a number of strategies that people can try to reduce their day-to-day impact. One matter on which there is not complete agreement is whether or not the best approach to managing memory difficulties is to try and restore the lost ability by exercises, or to try and think of ways to work around the difficulties. The generally accepted consensus of opinion is that to see a clinically significant effect in humans, the better approach is compensation rather than restoration (see Chapter 2).

Although that means that practising a specific task isn't going to generally make your memory better, that certainly does not mean that there's no point practising specific tasks if you want to get better at that task. For example, if someone needs to learn how to transfer from a wheelchair onto a bed, then practising is a good way to learn it; it will make use of procedural memory, which often remains intact. Practising the transfer technique will make you better at that transfer, but it won't make you better able to remember your way to the gym. There isn't generalised improvement of memory.

A phrase that is often used to summarise a compensatory approach is 'take the strain off the brain', which means that if one particular skill is more difficult after a brain injury, then find an alternative way to do it to reduce the impact on daily life. There are a number of strategies that people with memory difficulties have found useful, and they're often described as being either external or internal memory strategies. External strategies involve the use of some sort of accessory, be that a diary or be it another person reminding you, while internal strategies are techniques that you can carry out in your head.

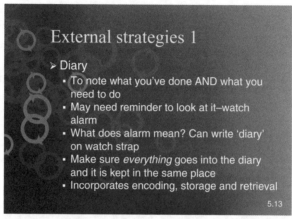

Slide 5.13

Perhaps the most obvious and commonly used external memory aid is a diary. One advantage of using a diary is that they are very common. Many people use diaries at work and outside work, so there's no particular stigma to using a diary and no need to feel self-conscious about using one. When people are having difficulties with remembering new information, there are two valuable ways in which a diary can be used.

Firstly, it can be used prospectively – looking forwards in time – so that you have a list of appointments or jobs you need to do that day and a note of what time they need doing. Secondly, the diary can be used retrospectively, that is, to record briefly things that have happened that are important to remember. As well as being an appointments list, a diary can also act as a journal of events. This can be of help in trying to manage the frustrations and distress of having a memory difficulty. People sometimes describe feeling 'lost in the present', as they find it harder to remember what is coming up in the future and harder to recall what happened the previous day. Even brief notes can be useful in alleviating some of that distress, as they can provide a little more context for the present and maybe allow for some more discussion of shared experiences with friends.

An obvious point to make is that it's all very well writing things down in a diary, but it's not going to help as much as it could if you forget that you have a diary or forget to look in it regularly. Ironically, this is particularly likely to be the case in the exact group of people who need it most. One potential solution is to combine the use of a diary with some sort of cue or prompt, such as the hourly time signal on a digital watch, or an alarm on a mobile phone or electronic organiser, which serves as a reminder to look in the diary.

For some people their memory difficulties can be so severe that it is hard to remember what the alarm represents, and so it can be useful to add another stage to the system, such as putting a sticker on the watch strap saying 'diary', or using the electronic organiser to remind you that the alarm means to look in your diary. This demonstrates the importance of making external memory strategies watertight, so the memory difficulties themselves don't reduce their utility.

Consistency is crucial to just about any memory strategy. As procedural memory can remain intact, it's important to set up routines and habits, as this will play to the common strength that people will have. Writing everything important in the diary and checking it at regular times is helpful. Never put it off saying 'I'll do it later', because that increases the chances that you will forget. In order to make the system work, the resources needed have to be available, which may mean carrying around a small pocket diary and pen all the time. If a larger diary at home is more practical, then it needs to be kept in the same place all the time and updated and referred to at consistent set times.

Using a diary quite neatly mimics the three stages of memory; the encoding stage is represented by writing information in the diary, the diary then stores it, and looking up the page of the diary correlates with retrieval.

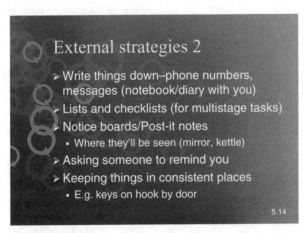

External strategies 2

- Write things down–phone numbers, messages (notebook/diary with you)
- Lists and checklists (for multistage tasks)
- Notice boards/Post-it notes
  - Where they'll be seen (mirror, kettle)
- Asking someone to remind you
- Keeping things in consistent places
  - E.g. keys on hook by door

5.14

Slide 5.14

There are several other external memory strategies, a lot of which will be common-sense approaches that many of the population will make use of to a greater or lesser degree. Obviously writing things down can be safer than trying to retain information in your head, and to ensure that this becomes a habit it can be useful for people with memory difficulties to carry a small notebook and pen around with them, and establish the habit of noting down things that they want to remember. Making lists of things to do or buy is also a common strategy employed by much of the population, and can be a big help with 'prospective' memory, that is remembering things that need to be done in the future.

Certain tasks involve a lot of separate stages. For example, when cooking a three-course meal, certain things need to start being cooked at certain times, and the order is very important to ensure that everything is ready at the right time. It can be helpful to write out a checklist beforehand to refer to, which can reduce the need to keep everything in mind at once, and so reduce the chances of forgetting a stage.

Reminder notes suffer from the same drawback as diaries, in that they are of little use if you forget to look at them. The more they 'jump out at you' the better, so it can be useful to put them in places where you can't miss them, for example on the kettle or on the shaving mirror, or somewhere else that forms part of your daily routine.

Asking someone else to remind you is a very valid and helpful external memory aid. Remember that one in four of the general population experiences memory lapses associated with some nuisance value, so there is not always necessarily any loss of face associated with asking someone to remind you.

'Losing things' was one of the three most common memory difficulties that the general population reported. Themes of consistency and habit can play a useful part here, as keeping things in the same place every time you put them down means that you are less likely to mislay them. Examples include keeping door keys on a hook by the door, always putting your wallet on a particular shelf or keeping your glasses in a certain designated spot. The old phrase 'don't put something down, put it away' can be a useful motto.

There's a list of external strategies that people have found helpful on the handout. It may be helpful to have a look through and pick one or maybe two that seem most relevant to any difficulties you're aware of and have a go at incorporating them into your routines. It may be the case that you are already using some of the external strategies. If they're not proving watertight, it may be that you can incorporate some extra consistency or an extra element into the systems you're using. It may also be the case that adopting one extra strategy as part of a routine (for example, always putting your keys in the same place when you get home, or checking your diary every time you have a cup of tea) can reduce the frequency of frustrating incidents that can have a cumulative effect on how you feel.

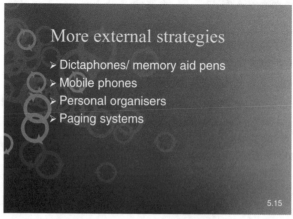

Slide 5.15

As technology develops, more gadgets become available that can be very useful as memory aids. It is now possible to buy pens that can record a short amount of speech, working in much the same way as a dictaphone. This means that when something arises that you know you will want to remember later (even if it's only by the time you reach the top of the stairs) you can record it by saying it out loud, and then remind yourself by playing it back when you need it. Mobile phones and palm-top computers can be set to provide reminders, and use can be made of paging systems to have reminders sent at set times.

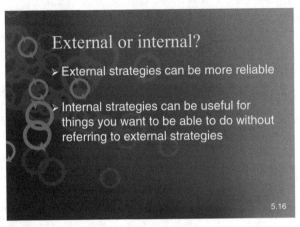

Slide 5.16

Although external memory strategies can be a very reliable approach if used consistently, there are often things that we want to remember and bring to mind without referring to a list or a notebook. Examples might include people's names, addresses, or number codes for alarms or cashpoints. This is where internal memory strategies can come in useful for some people. It is worth noting that applying an internal strategy in itself involves extra effort and for some people this approach can be unhelpful, particularly if there are a range of difficulties with other skills such as concentration or planning.

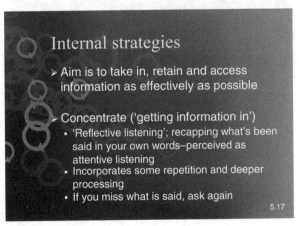

Slide 5.17

As with the external strategies, internal strategies aim to increase the efficiency of taking in, storing and retrieving information. The first stage is heavily affected by concentration. If we're not concentrating on something, then the encoding of the information being presented can be poor. One way of increasing the efficiency of encoding is to 'process' the information that's coming in in a deliberate way. One way to do that is to consider or manipulate the information in a way that requires you to process it more deeply. A useful approach to try is called 'reflective listening'. When someone says something to you, you essentially recap it in your own words. For example, if a friend says 'I'm going to France for a fortnight with my sister and her husband', you could reply by saying something like, 'so you're off to the continent with the family – are you looking forward to it?' As well as meaning you've processed the information to the extent that you have extracted its meaning and organised it in your own way, there is also the advantage of some repetition. It can seem that this would be very odd in conversations (and of course people will think it strange if you just parrot everything they say), but done sensibly it is in fact perceived as being very attentive and showing that you are listening and understanding what is being said. Because of this, this technique is in fact commonly recommended in counselling training, where it is called 'empathic listening', with the counsellor reflecting back the emotional gist of what has just been said, for example, 'it sounds like that was very upsetting for you'.

On a more basic level, if you miss what someone has said, or it simply doesn't register for some reason, then it's often simplest to ask them to repeat it rather than to feel embarrassed and struggle through the rest of the conversation. Saying for example, 'I'm sorry I didn't catch your name' and then repeating it aloud when you're told again can sometimes save awkwardness later on. Remembering the fact that one in four people might have to do the same can be useful in giving extra confidence to ask.

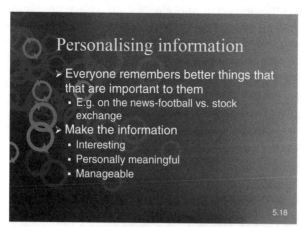

Slide 5.18

We've mentioned already that the nature of what we're trying to remember has a big impact on how well we remember it. If something is interesting to us, and relevant to us, then we're likely to remember it better. This is something we can use to our advantage by making information more interesting and more personally meaningful, as well as by organising it so that it is more manageable.

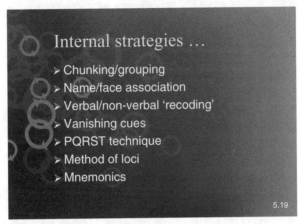

Slide 5.19

There are a number of internal memory strategies, some of which we can practise in this session. First of all, have a look at this next slide for a few seconds and try and remember what's on the shopping list.

Slide 5.20

[CLICK BACK TO SLIDE 19 SO THAT SLIDE 20 IS NOT VISIBLE.] How many of the items of the shopping list can you remember? [ASK GROUP MEMBERS TO SHOUT OUT.]

Now have a look again at the same list . . . [CLICK FORWARDS TO SLIDE 21].

Slide 5.21

[CLICK BACK TO SLIDE 19 SO SLIDES 20/21 AREN'T VISIBLE.] Now how many can you remember? [ASK GROUP MEMBERS TO SHOUT OUT].

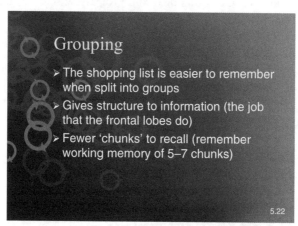

Slide 5.22

It's usually easier to remember more when material is structured into meaningful groups. Putting a structure like that onto otherwise random information is very similar to one of the jobs that the frontal lobes do, which is arranging information so that it is more manageable and organised. This can increase the ease with which we can encode information in the first place and subsequently retrieve it when we need to.

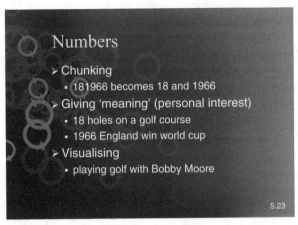

Slide 5.23

Another example of imposing structure onto information in order to make it manageable is commonly called 'chunking', and it can be combined with some other internal strategies. If we need to remember a number, be it a telephone number or a number for an alarm system keypad, one helpful step is to break down the number of chunks of information that we have to deal with. For example, a six-digit entry code of 181966 can be split into just two chunks of the number 18 and the year 1966. There is an overlap here with making information personally meaningful; for someone who was keen on sport, 18 might make them think of a golf course, while 1966 might make them think of the year that England won the football World Cup. For some people, those examples would be no help at all as they're not interested in sport, and that serves to make the point that to be helpful it has to be personalised, so that the chunks are meaningful to you as an individual. For other people, it may be that 1966 represents the year they were married, or the year that the Beatles' *Yellow Submarine* was released. The key is to tailor the information to your own personal interests, because we all remember information that's meaningful and interesting to us better than information that isn't.

If someone has had an injury or condition affecting the left side of the brain, it may be that they have particular difficulty with remembering words, but their non-verbal or visual memory is just as good as ever. Numbers tend to fall into the 'words' category, and so would be affected by this (Aggleton, 1997). If they wanted to remember this code, we can play to their strengths by transforming verbal information into non-verbal information. Visualisation, or mental imagery, can work well in these circumstances. A mental image for 18 and 1966 might be Bobby Moore playing golf. Once again, the importance of personal interest is apparent here, as not everyone will know that Bobby Moore was England captain when we won the world cup in 1966. That image can also be transformed into a reminder picture placed next to the keypad (such as a sketch of a footballer in a red shirt using the world cup as a golf club), which would cue in the person who thought of it but wouldn't necessarily allow anyone else to work out the code. One general rule of thumb in the use of mental imagery is that the more bizarre the image, the more memorable it is.

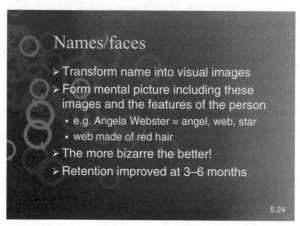

Slide 5.24

A similar idea has been shown to work extremely well with the very common and embarrassing problem of meeting someone that you know and being unable to remember their name. The trick here is to transform their name into visual images in the same way as we did with the numbers, and then form one overall mental image that involves the elements of their name as well as a physical characteristic from their appearance. A commonly used example involves a lady with long red hair called Angela Webster (Wilson, 1987). The name Angela Webster can be turned into images by breaking it down into parts; an angel, a web and a star. The next step is to create one mental image involving these features and her main physical characteristic of long red hair. Hence we can arrive at an image of a web made up of red hair, with an angel and a star trapped in it. [USE WHITEBOARD/FLIPCHART TO ILLUSTRATE THIS PROCESS.]

It can sound quite strange to suggest doing this, but the evidence does indicate that even up to six months later there can be an advantage (Wilson, 1987). There are some drawbacks in that there is the risk that you'll call everyone you meet who has long red hair 'Angela Webster', but it can be a very useful approach to help remembering the names of people who you know you will encounter frequently.

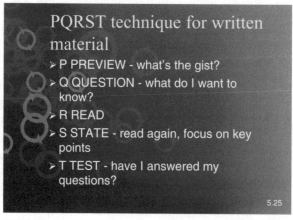

Slide 5.25

The next technique is aimed at helping to remember written information. It's derived from exam revision techniques, and has good supporting evidence to show that it really does help (Wilson & Moffat, 1992). It requires a fair bit of effort and practice, and you certainly wouldn't use it for everything you came across when you were reading, but for important information that you want to commit to memory it can be effective. It's quite useful to practise this technique with newspaper articles as they lend themselves quite well to this approach. [USE NEWSPAPER ARTICLE AS DEMONSTRATION OF APPLYING PQRST].

In the PQRST technique each of the letters P, Q, R, S and T stand for a stage to go through. 'R' stands for 'read', so it's clear that there are a couple of stages to go through before even reading the information. First of all, 'P' stands for 'preview'. This means that you want to get an idea of the gist of what the material is about to give it some context. In a newspaper article, this can be easily achieved by reading the main headline and any of the sub-headlines or pictures throughout. The next letter, 'Q' stands for 'question'; what is it that you would want to know by the time you've finished reading the article? If the story were to be discussed later in the day with a group of people, what would you want to know about it so that you didn't feel left out? Your questions will only be based on a knowledge of the gist of the information, as we haven't read it yet. This is a key stage of the PQRST technique, because it involves tailoring the material to your own interests or curiosity. In doing so you're making it more interesting and more personally meaningful rather than it being just words on a page.

The next stage, 'R', is to read the information. The stage after that is 'S', which stands for 'state'. This involves stating the information back to yourself as you re-read it trying to link the content in with the questions that you asked yourself. Finally, 'T' stands for 'test'; test yourself to see if you are now able to answer the questions that you wanted to know the answers to. Sometimes, of course, a newspaper article won't include what you particularly wanted to know. There is a dual benefit to be gained from using the PQRST technique; as well as increasing the depth to which you process the information in order to make it more personally relevant and meaningful, it also includes some repetition.

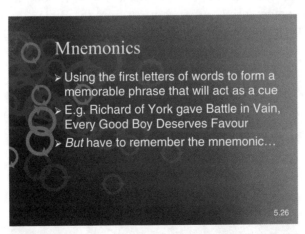

Slide 5.26

Mnemonics are used very commonly in daily life to help people remember certain things. They crop up in schools, universities and in work settings. One example is the well-known

'Richard of York' mnemonic, which gives the colours of the rainbow, as each word of the sentence 'Richard of York gave battle in vain' begins with the first letter of the colours of the rainbow in order (red, orange, yellow and so on). Similarly, many music teachers make their pupils learn the phrase 'every good boy deserves favour', which gives you the musical notes on the staff lines when you're looking at sheet music (EGBDF).

Mnemonics are often not so useful for people who have memory difficulties, because it requires having to remember the mnemonic itself. This can be as difficult as remembering the original information, so it tends not to be used so much in practice.

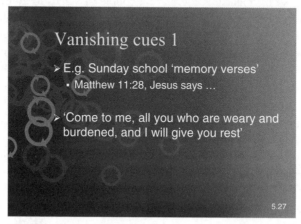

Slide 5.27

The next strategy is called 'vanishing cues' and is another useful way to learn short pieces of verbal information that you want to keep in mind, for example addresses. Commonly, people are familiar with this strategy if they ever used to attend Sunday School, as this was traditionally used to learn verses from the Bible. Each week there would be a 'memory verse' from the Bible, and 'vanishing cues' was a way of making it easier to learn. We can practice this technique using one such verse from the Bible. [GROUP MEMBERS READ TOGETHER OUT LOUD THE BIBLE VERSE FROM SLIDE 5.27, THEN PRESENT NEXT SLIDE.]

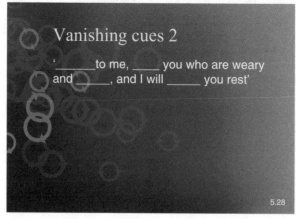

Slide 5.28

[PRESENT THE FOLLOWING SLIDES, WITH ATTENDEES READING OUT THE WHOLE SENTENCE EACH TIME, CLICKING BACK TO THE PREVIOUS SLIDE BRIEFLY IF NECESSARY.] It's clear at this stage why this approach is called 'vanishing cues'; as we proceed there will be fewer words on each slide, meaning fewer cues to the content.

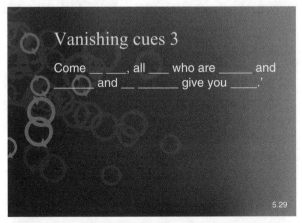

Slide 5.29

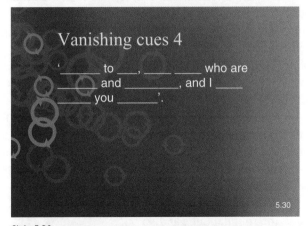

Slide 5.30

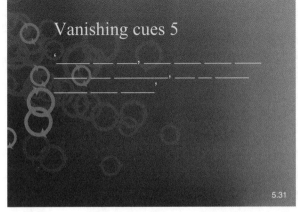

Slide 5.31

[AT LEAST SOME OF THE GROUP MAY BE ABLE TO HAVE REPEATED THE WHOLE VERSE FROM MEMORY BY THIS STAGE, THUS DEMONSTRATING THE EFFICACY OF THIS APPROACH.]

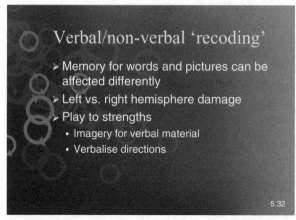

Slide 5.32

As has already been mentioned, the two different sides of the brain are involved with memory for different sorts of information. The left side of the brain tends to be more involved with language and verbal memory, for example remembering people's names or an address, while the right side of the brain tends to be more involved with non-verbal material, such as remembering faces or how to get somewhere.

If just one side of the brain is injured by a stroke or a head injury, for example, then there can be difficulties with either verbal or non-verbal memory while the other type remains pretty much intact. The general principle is to 'play to your strengths'. For example, if remembering names is difficult, a useful strategy would involve turning the words into pictures that are easier to remember. To remember a code for a keypad, it can be easier to remember the spatial order in which to press the keys rather than the numbers themselves.

Similarly, if non-verbal memory is more difficult, it can help to turn the visual information into words. Instead of remembering visually which way to walk to reach your intended goal, it can help to turn the route into verbal instructions, such as 'first left, second right, straight ahead at the roundabout', and so on.

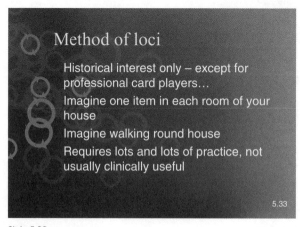

Slide 5.33

The 'method of loci' is an internal memory strategy that has been around since at least Roman times. The Romans used to gather in their meeting places and listen to orators making speeches. The orators were the equivalent of pop stars nowadays, and to be thought of as any good they had to deliver their speech without referring to any notes; using notes was seen as being rather amateurish. In order to achieve this they used the 'method of loci'; 'loci' is the Latin for 'places', and the reason for the name will become clear. The speakers would imagine the layout of their own house, with all of its rooms and particular places within it. Then they'd create a mental visual image of the first point that they wanted to make in their speech, and imagine placing that image in the first room that they'd go into when they walked into their house. They did the same for each subsequent point in the speech, until they had a range of images in various imagined locations throughout their house. When it came to giving the speech, the speakers would imagine walking round the house in their mind, and so would be reminded of each point they wanted to make as they spotted the images as they walked round the house in their mind.

It takes a lot of practice to do well, but can be very effective, and is one of the common tricks used by professional 'memory men' who remember packs of cards and phone directories. It is unlikely to be useful for people who have memory difficulties because in itself it takes a lot of planning skills to be effective and is quite effortful; it is largely included for interest's sake.

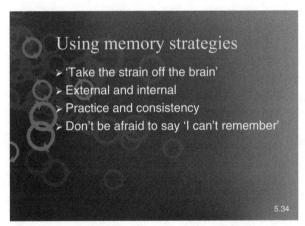

Slide 5.34

In summary, the most effective way to reduce the day-to-day impact of memory difficulties is to find ways to work around the particular aspect of memory that is more difficult, thus 'taking the strain off the brain'. This can be achieved either by using external accessories such as diaries, lists, or other people, or by using internal strategies such as chunking, grouping, or manipulating information to play to your strengths.

The key to all of these strategies is practice and consistency; the more you can establish some of these approaches into habits, the more likely they are to be helpful. It's also important to appreciate that no one has a perfect memory; it is entirely possible to say that you can't remember something without being seen as unusual.

Memory

Some useful facts:

1. Up to *25%* of the general population say their memory can be a nuisance.
2. Memory isn't just one thing, which is either 'good' or 'bad'; there are different types of memory, and a brain injury often affects some but not all of them. This means that it's often possible to reduce the impact of memory difficulties on daily life by playing to your strengths.
3. Most commonly, difficulties arise when trying to make *new* memories (i.e. learning new information), but memories for events before the brain injury remain intact.
4. It's easier to *recognise* things than to *recall* them without any clues. If someone you know has difficulties with memory, it can be helpful to bear in mind that just because they recognise you when they see you, don't assume that they can remember things like your name, let alone all the details of your last conversation.
5. One very important distinction is between memory for *words* and memory for *images.* Usually the left side of the brain deals with verbal memory (e.g. remembering something you've been told or have read), and the right side deals with visual memory (e.g. remembering how to get somewhere). A stroke commonly only affects one side or the other, which means that one type of memory may well be just as good as ever.
6. There are three stages to making a new memory:

   Encoding – getting the information in
   Storage – keeping it there
   Retrieval – getting at it when you want it

Sometimes only one stage is affected, and this can affect which strategies may be most useful for you.

Memory strategies

The most useful approach is not to try and train you memory, for example by practising learning lists. This can be useful if you want to memorise a particular list, but it won't generalise and make your memory for other things better.

The key is to play to your strengths and use either external strategies (using aids like diaries, written lists, etc.) and/or internal strategies (tricks you can do in your head without any aids) to try and compensate for areas of difficulty.

External strategies

- Diary: can be used in two ways – to note things that you have to do, and those things that you've done and want to remember. May need a prompt/routine to look at it (e.g. hourly alarm). Consistency is crucial – where's it kept? (back pocket? handbag? by the kettle?)
- Alarms and notes
- Checklists
- Post-it notes (where they'll be seen – mirror, kettle. . .)
- Asking someone to remind you
- Keeping things in consistent places (e.g. keys on hook by door).

Internal strategies
'Re-coding' information

If your strength is for verbal memory, then practise turning visual information into verbal information and you'll be using the stronger side of your brain. For example, when trying to remember a route, verbalise it as 'first left, second right, etc.' If your strength is for visual memory, practise turning words into mental images (e.g. imagine a chicken drinking wine if you wanted to remember that you'd ordered 'coq au vin'). The more bizarre, the more memorable!

Reflective listening

Helps with the 'encoding' stage for spoken information, as there's some repetition and also it requires deeper 'processing' of the information. Essentially, try recapping what's been said in your own words; it's perceived as very attentive listening when used sparingly.

PQRST

Helps with the 'encoding' stage for written information, as there's some repetition and it also requires deeper 'processing' of the information. It makes information more personally meaningful as you've put your own structure on it.

P Preview – what's the gist of the text?
Q Question – what do I want to know when I've read it?
R Read it.
S State it – read it again, linking it back to your questions.
T Test yourself – can I answer my questions?

Structuring information

Structuring aids with the encoding and retrieval stages; that is, in putting structure onto information it mimics what the frontal lobes would be doing anyway. Sort lists into groups according to certain characteristics (e.g. what letter they start with, how big they are, or whatever works).

'Chunking' information

The smaller the number of pieces of information that the brain has to remember, the easier it is. If you have to remember a 6-digit number, split it up into chunks, e.g. 181966 can become 18 and 1966. If the chunks have any meaning to them (e.g. 1966 England won the World Cup), even better.

Names and faces

1. Transform the name into visual images (e.g. Angela Webster becomes an angel, a web and a star).
2. Identify a physical characteristic of the person that will be your prompt (e.g. red hair)
3. Form a mental image involving all these features (e.g. an angel and a star caught in a web made of red hair).

It sounds strange, but it works (up to six months later in the studies). It involves both verbal and non-verbal memory, and requires deeper processing and structuring.

'Vanishing cues'

This can be useful for learning verbal information that you don't want to have to look up, for example, addresses. Write out the address, then write it out with more and more words missing. Then go through them in order, writing in the blanks until you have written out the whole address from memory.

Summary

Play to your strengths.
Use external and internal strategies.
Don't be afraid to say 'I can't remember'.

Some examples to practise

(N.B. practising these will make you better at applying the strategy effectively rather than improving your memory itself). If you can find more relevant material to practise with, go for it!

Try grouping these lists:
cheese peas mangoes chicken milk pears beef apples duck grapes eggs apples pork bananas turkey cream oranges
Germany England Italy Zimbabwe Ireland Sweden Wales Norway Ghana Denmark France Sudan
Peter Steven Amy Bernard Sarah Paul Belinda Bob Polly Anna Simon Bertha Patrick

Try chunking these numbers:
485320 936574 753402 853760

Try this 'vanishing cues' exercise:
Peter Molyneux, 18 Nightingale Drive, Sunbury-on-Thames, Middlesex, TW19 7TS.

Peter Molyneux, 18 _____ Drive, Sunbury-on- _____, _____, TW19 7TS.

Peter _____, __ Nightingale Drive, _____-on- Thames, _____, TW19 7TS.

_____ _____, 18 _____ _____, Sunbury-__- _____, _____, ____ 7TS.

Peter Molyneux, ___ Nightingale _____, _____ -on- _____, _____, ____ 7TS.

____ , _____, _____ Drive, _____-on- _____, _____, TW19 ___.

_____ _____, __ _____ ___, _____-__- _____, _____, ____

_____.

Traditionally used to memorise Bible verses – plenty of material to practise with there.

PQRST
Get a paper and practise with some short articles.

Preview	What's the headline? What's the gist of the story?
Question	What do I want to find out from reading this? What would I want to tell someone if they asked me what I was reading?
Read	
State	Link back what you've read to your own questions.
Test	Can I answer the questions I asked myself?

Names and Faces
What mental image could you make for . . .?

    Donald Carpenter who wears big glasses

    Jemma King who wears big earrings

    Russell Jackson who has a goatee beard

You can try other examples from people's names and pictures in the paper.

How would you turn this visual information into words?
(e.g. 'a circle with a line through it')
φ   ϖ   Ԋ

How would you turn this verbal information into images?
'The bins will be collected on Tuesday next week.'
'Pick up some bread and milk on your way home from work.'

Chapter 6
Executive Function

Comments about material

For the purposes of simplicity within this session, the range of skills that is classically included within the domain of 'executive function' is described as being linked with the frontal lobes. This is clearly a simplification, as various studies have linked executive skills with disparate brain areas including the cerebellum (Schmahmann & Sherman, 1998). In acquired brain injury settings, the frequency of injuries to the frontal lobes and resultant dysexecutive syndromes suggests that such a simplification is warranted for the purposes in hand, although of course there may be attendees for whom the provision of additional information is appropriate.

Any attempt to describe the skills encompassed by the term 'executive function', ground them in functional examples and make suggestions about their management, all within the confines of a single session is almost certain to have its limitations. Attempting to rehearse any management strategies over and above this seems impractical within the same session. Indeed, one established and evaluated group-based approach to the management of executive dysfunction takes the form of a course of sessions running twice weekly for 8–10 weeks, and also includes some individual input (Evans, 2001), in order to comprehensively cover education, strategy rehearsal, and generalisation of strategies to functional tasks.

The session described in this chapter is weighted rather more towards information provision than specific management techniques, and is in some ways designed more with family members in mind than other sessions might be. Some of the management strategies mentioned would very likely need further input for attendees to apply effectively. One reason for this is that the concept of executive function is generally less familiar to people than the more tangible concepts of memory and concentration, and as such more explanation is required to explain changes that may have resulted from an acquired brain injury or neurological condition. Secondly, changes in executive skills can have marked implications on social behaviour, and hence improving family/carer understanding of the reasons for this is an important intervention in itself.

This session has a slightly different structure to it than the other sessions. While it begins, as do the others, with some of the 'theory' in order to provide a framework, use is then made of some descriptions of behaviour (in the form of fictitious quotations from carers) with the aim of embedding the theoretical information firmly within functional examples. Each such example is followed by an explanation of the behaviour in terms of cognition, and a general recommendation to attribute such behaviour changes to 'situational' rather than 'dispositional' factors (Ross, 1977) and to adopt an agreed approach to their management where practical.

Subjectively, describing the effects on behaviour of executive dysfunction can often feel very awkward when the group includes patients and/or their loved ones. This is likely to reflect the extent to which social behaviour is associated with concepts of 'personality', and hence drawing attention to any changes to social behaviour can be perceived as extremely threatening to the sense of self of attendees. This is a sensitive topic, and one that it can be tempting to avoid. In some (indeed many) circumstances, individual information provision will be indicated, but it is the case that it is precisely this area of cognition that can have the biggest detrimental effect on carers' quality of life, and there will be benefits from the normalisation and validation of this experience in a group setting. Once it is acknowledged that the information is important to provide to family members, carers or staff, then there would need to be a very clear reason not to provide the information to the 'patient' themselves.

Practical suggestions for managing the potentially sensitive information include avoiding the oft-used notion of 'personality change' and instead describing changes in terms of specific cognitive skills that may be inefficient. This shift in emphasis steers away from an 'all or nothing' conceptualisation of cognition in which impairment is seen as a global loss of self, and can foster a more realistic appreciation of specific difficulties that may seem more manageable and less threatening.

When providing staff training, highlighting the difference between attributing behaviour change to dispositional and situational factors (Ross, 1977) can be a very useful approach (see Chapter 2).

It can also be helpful to emphasise the extent to which executive function fractionates, such that by no means all the features mentioned in this session will relate to all individuals.

Emotional lability is included here rather than in the 'thoughts and feelings' session as it sits well with other involuntary behavioural manifestations of brain injury.

Material to include

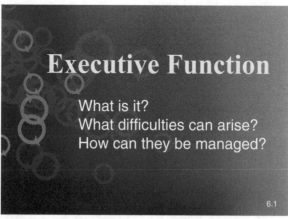

Executive Function

What is it?
What difficulties can arise?
How can they be managed?

6.1

Slide 6.1

While many people have a basic idea about what we mean by 'memory' or 'concentration', this particular topic can seem a little less familiar. Generally people haven't come across the term 'executive function', but it's one piece of jargon that can be quite helpful because it sums up quite well the kind of skills we'll be considering. Just as the term itself doesn't tell us straight away what it relates to in the way that 'memory' or 'concentration' do, the effects of any difficulties with executive function after an injury to the brain can be quite subtle, and can seem rather strange without a knowledge of the reasons for them.

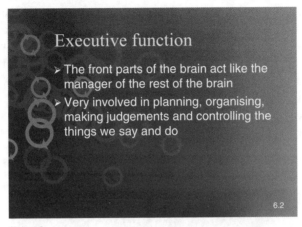

Slide 6.2

The front parts of the brain just behind the forehead are most involved in the range of skills we'll be considering in this session. It can be helpful to think about these front parts of the brain as being like the manager of the rest of the brain. There may be parts of the brain just behind your ears that remember information, and there may be parts of the brain right at the back that are involved in seeing things, but it's the front parts of the brain – the frontal lobes – that tell these other bits what to remember and what to look at. It's very much that role of planning and organising that the front parts of the brain are involved in, as well as being very involved in making judgements and controlling the way that we act.

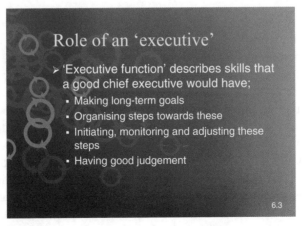

Slide 6.3

The reason why we're using the jargon phrase 'executive function' is because the frontal lobes are crucial for a lot of the skills that a chief executive of a company would have, so it's a good comparison to make (Powell, 1994). For example, the chief executive of a company would make plans for where he or she wants the company to be in 10 years' time. Then they'd work out what the first step towards that goal would be, perhaps planning where the company needed to be in 6 months' time. They'd make the necessary arrangements for this short-term plan to be put into action, and they'd make sure that they kept an eye on how things were progressing, to be sure that things were staying on track. They would be vigilant for any difficulties that arose preventing the targets from being achieved, and they would deal with those difficulties in order to keep things moving towards the overall goal. This might mean changing the plans, so thinking flexibly and demonstrating good judgement is an important element. Overall, the chief executive is vital in making sure that planned outcomes actually happen, and that's not a bad way to think about what executive functions are.

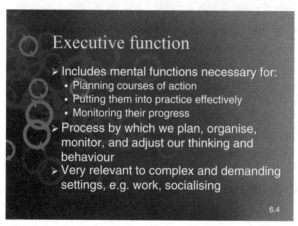

Slide 6.4

All this planning and working towards goals can be summarised into three stages; planning courses of action, implementing them and monitoring their progress (Evans, 2002a). Many day-to-day activities, particularly ones that aren't routine and familiar, rely on the combination of these abilities. For example, when we make a cup of tea we have an overall goal of having a drink. There are some in-between goals that need to be achieved along the way, such as boiling the water. Even before that, we might need to fill the kettle. If the kettle won't boil for some reason, then we might need to take stock of the situation, monitor what's going on and ascertain what the difficulty is – perhaps the kettle might not be plugged in. Then that obstacle needs to be addressed by plugging it in before we can move forwards towards the overall goal. Even very basic tasks can turn out to be made up of a number of stages that need to be carried out in the right sequence. To step it up a level, consider the example of cooking Sunday lunch for the whole family. That takes a lot of planning to make sure all the vegetables are done at the same time as the meat, and the pudding's ready shortly after that. To manage a task like that, the frontal lobes have to be working hard in order to think ahead, plan what order to do things in, start the individual tasks at the right time, keep an eye on how everything's going, make adjustments if something is cooking too quickly, make ongoing judgements about priorities and make decisions about when things are cooked sufficiently.

From the nature of the skills that we've seen the frontal lobes are involved with, it may already be apparent that if they aren't working as effectively as they might, difficulties can arise in situations that require decision making, problem solving, making plans and prioritising. This is particularly true in situations in which there is a lot going on at once. That tends to be exactly the situation people can find themselves in at work, with multiple demands, deadlines and time pressures. Often it's the work environment that is particularly challenging for people who have had an injury that affects their executive function. Social settings can also make demands on executive functions, for example making decisions about how to act based on the context and who is present, in a situation where there may be many people talking at once. It can be in social settings that difficulties with executive function can become apparent, albeit in sometimes quite subtle ways.

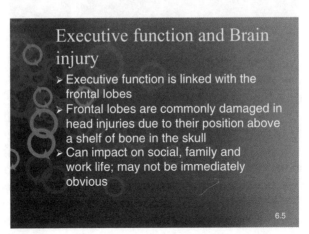

Slide 6.5

Difficulties with executive function are relatively common after injuries to the brain. One reason for this is that it is the frontal lobes that are particularly associated with these executive functions (although other parts of the brain are involved too). These frontal lobes sit on a shelf of bone just behind the forehead, and the inside surface of the skull is quite rough in this area. If there is a sudden deceleration such as might occur in a car accident, and the skull stops moving but the brain doesn't, then the delicate front parts of the brain will collide with the hard, rough inside of the skull, causing injury to exactly the parts of the brain that are most commonly involved with executive function. It's also the case that some neurological conditions involve the frontal lobes of the brain, and a stroke can affect the blood supply to the front parts of the brain causing injury there. Whatever the cause, injury to the front parts of the brain commonly affect executive functions, and can have marked effects on social skills, family life and in the work setting. As with other skills with which the brain is involved such as remembering things and maintaining concentration, it's often the case that the individual who has had the injury is just as intelligent as ever, but has a particular difficulty with specific tasks.

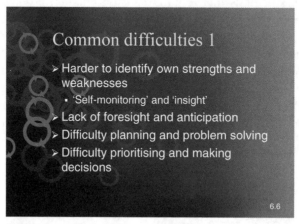

Slide 6.6

One thing we know about executive function is that in fact it includes a whole range of different skills, such that many aspects of it can remain intact while others can be less efficient. Here's a list of some of the difficulties that can arise, and you'll see that although there are many of them, they all relate to the kind of job that a chief executive would have.

One important element is that it can be particularly hard for the person who has had an injury to the brain to be aware of their own strengths and weaknesses in their changed circumstances. That's certainly not necessarily because they're stubborn or difficult, but it can relate to a difficulty with the role that the front parts of the brain have in monitoring situations. Just like the chief executive who keeps a check on progress and identifies what is working well for the company and what might be going badly, the frontal lobes are important in 'self-monitoring'. They keep tabs on our own behaviours and skills, and recognise our strengths and weaknesses. If the frontal lobes of the brain are injured, and some skills do become more difficult, ironically it can then be difficult for that person to be aware that some things are now harder for them. Difficulties of this nature are often called difficulties with 'insight' into the condition. When there is a difficulty with insight, it can be very frustrating for the person concerned when health professionals keep mentioning the difficulties and any limitations it might have on, for example, driving or going back to work.

Planning ahead is a hallmark of a good chief executive, and incorporates the ability to think beyond the 'here and now', and be prepared for the future. At a basic level, an example of this might involve making sure that you've bought all the ingredients you need for the

Sunday lunch, and that you've got everything out of the cupboards that you need to do the preparation. This planning skill can be very relevant to consider when people are about to go home from hospital after an injury to the brain. It is important to take steps to make sure that people will have the support they need to be able to carry out the complicated tasks that form part of daily life, even the ones that are normally taken for granted. If someone is struggling with this sort of skill and they go home without support around them, it can be very dangerous. If there is also a difficulty with insight, it can be very difficult for people to accept such support (for example, asking for help when going on a complex public transport trip) because it can be seen as unnecessary. Sometimes it's only when the more subtle difficulties like planning ahead and solving unexpected problems do arise in day-to-day life that insight into their presence increases. This is one reason for accepting any help that there is available initially while this process of discovering the effects of executive difficulties is still going on. Sometimes it remains difficult to appreciate one's own difficulties, and it can be very frustrating to have people offering help and advice when you don't think you need it. It can cause a lot of friction, but it also presents obvious safety concerns if someone is attempting to do things that are currently beyond their realistic abilities.

Just as the chief executive of a company makes long-term goals and thinks carefully through the consequences of potential courses of action, the frontal lobes weigh up the pros and cons of our own actions and help us arrive at a reasoned decision as to whether or not we should proceed. For example, if we're unable to bear any weight on one of our legs because of our condition, we'd consider whether or not it was safe to stand up and walk across the room before we actually did it. Our decision may or may not be safe, but in the usual course of events we'd at least weigh up any potential dangers and include them in our decision making. This skill of decision making based on thinking through potential risks and consequences is another aspect of executive function. If the frontal lobes aren't working at 100%, then sometimes people can act without full consideration of the consequences. It's often described as acting in an 'impulsive' way, without taking the risks or dangers into account.

Another related aspect of executive function is to do with making choices. An example would be deciding how to travel to a destination, with a range of options including the train, the bus or driving the car. When we make a decision like that, we tend to base it on the advantages and disadvantages of each option. In this example, these might include cost, time and personal preference. If the frontal lobes are finding it harder to weigh up the pros and cons of each option, then one result is that decision making can become much more difficult. One approach in trying to manage difficulties of this sort is to try and consciously work through each of the steps that would normally be considered automatically. This would involve very methodically considering each option's advantages and disadvantages, perhaps even writing them out before arriving at any conclusions. This kind of difficulty can become very relevant in decision making relating to life-changing decisions, such as where to live, getting married, or accepting or refusing medical treatment. If, for example, someone is refusing to have a medical treatment, then it is important to know that they are able to appreciate the consequences of refusing it. If that isn't the case because executive function difficulties are affecting decision making and insight, then it can start off complicated discussions about whether or not someone is capable of taking such a decision for themselves.

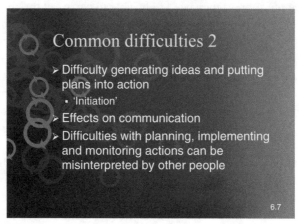

Slide 6.7

Another task which comes under the heading of 'executive function' relates to the ability to put plans into action. This is often called 'initiation'. If there is a difficulty with this, it can mean that although somebody may be quite capable of carrying out a task, they lack the ability to begin doing it and can need some prompting to begin. This type of difficulty can make it hard for people to act on information that they are told, or to modify their behaviour in response to new information; for example, if they've been told that something is now kept in a new place it can be hard to stop looking for it in the old place.

It's often very apparent that these skills to do with planning actions, implementing them and monitoring how well they're going, are reflected in the way that people speak. For example, it can be harder to speak fluently and keep track of the conversation without losing sight of the point that you were aiming to make. It can be harder to use or understand subtle hidden meanings in jokes, or to use or understand metaphors or comparisons, because it takes some monitoring skills to pick up that the words aren't intended to be taken at face value, and then some interpretation to see beyond the literal meaning. It can be harder to initiate conversations and then to adjust responses to the changing demands of a conversation depending on who else is present.

These functions of the brain clearly have a marked impact on our interactions with other people, and this makes it very important for other people to be aware of them. Some of the effects of executive function difficulties are easy to misinterpret, and without adequate knowledge other people can assume that the person who has executive function difficulties might be lazy, stubborn or even drunk. It's crucial, therefore, for people to know about this particular aspect of brain injury. In order to try and make it as relevant to real-life as possible, we'll go through some examples, many of which can be thought of in terms of a difficulty with either planning, implementing or monitoring speech or actions.

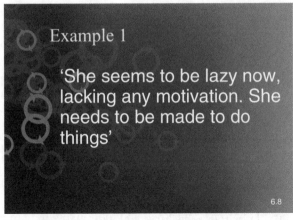

Slide 6.8

The first example is a comment made by the husband of a lady who had had a stroke; he commented that his wife seemed to be lazy now, lacked any motivation, and he had to work quite hard to make her do anything.

It's easy to imagine that if someone thinks that their wife is being lazy, it's quite likely that they'd feel angry and frustrated with them, it might lead to arguments and might well have a negative effect on their relationship.

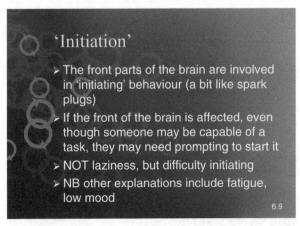

Slide 6.9

An alternative possible explanation for the lady's change in behaviour relates to the effects on the brain of the stroke. This is also relevant for head injuries and other neurological conditions too. The front parts of the brain are particularly involved in 'initiating' or starting behaviour. They can be compared in that respect to the spark plugs in a car, which need to spark in order to start the engine. If this 'initiating' function of the brain is not working as efficiently as usual, then it can be much more difficult for an individual to begin carrying out a task, even though they may be entirely capable of doing it once they've started. They may well need some explicit prompting or instruction to start. It's easy to see how this can be mistaken for laziness. It's also easy to see what a difference knowing the alternative explanation might have on the attitudes of people close to the person who is having difficulties with initiation. Their attitude might change from being angry, resentful and confused to being more understanding and helpful, which might encourage working together to manage the difficulty.

The change in attitudes and behaviour that can result from a different understanding of a situation can be very marked. That's easily demonstrated by a study carried out in America back in 1980, in which people were asked how they would respond if they came across a man lying in the street (Weiner, 1980). Some people were told that the man was drunk, and many of them thought that he only had himself to blame, weren't sympathetic towards him and weren't very likely to help him. Some other people were told that the man was ill, and these people were more likely to be concerned and more likely to help him out. This study demonstrates the importance of understanding some of the features related to executive skills that can have a marked impact on people's behaviour and social interactions. Having some knowledge of the topics we're covering in this session can go some way towards reducing unnecessary friction at a time when things may be difficult enough already.

Of course it's important to acknowledge that it isn't always a clear picture. Sometimes there may well be other explanations for why somebody isn't carrying out a task, and such explanations can include the fatigue which is very common when the brain has been affected in any way, or feeling depressed, or on some occasions – just as in day-to-day life without any injury to the brain – just not wanting to do something. It can also be the case that certain tasks can be more anxiety provoking due to other current difficulties, for example walking outdoors due to difficulties with balance, and this can be mistaken for lack of motivation (Riley, 2005).

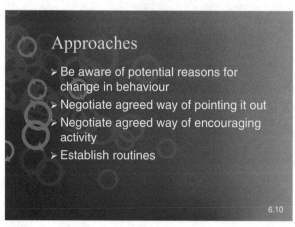

Slide 6.10

In managing such difficulties, the first step is for all parties concerned to be aware of the difficulty, as this can make it less likely that a difficulty with initiation will be mistaken for laziness and so lead to an argument. The second step, which is going to be common to most of the other examples that we'll cover, is to tackle it as a team wherever possible. We mentioned 'insight' earlier on, and it may be that if someone has trouble initiating actions, then they may also have difficulty in recognising that this is a new problem for them. In that case it may need to be pointed out in order for an activity to be started. It is important to negotiate how this will be done, so that there is a mutually acceptable prompt rather than something that feels like a nag or a complaint. That will involve some discussion between all the parties involved, and requires an understanding of the nature of the difficulties. That is the reason why, although it can feel awkward bringing up some of these difficulties that can seem very personal, it is important that we do acknowledge them. By giving you the information it can help you and those close to you plan the best way to mention any difficulties when they arise and the best way to manage them, for example by giving an agreed encouraging phrase rather than saying 'stop being so lazy'.

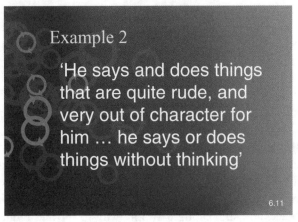

Slide 6.11

The mother of a young man who had sustained a head injury commented that 'he says and does things that are quite rude, and very out of character for him . . . he says or does things without thinking'. This was clearly very upsetting for the whole family, and it represented a big change from the way that the young man had previously tended to behave.

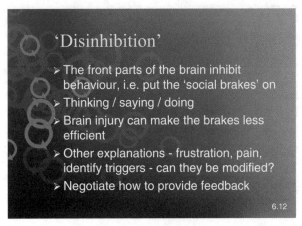

Slide 6.12

Changes such as this are relatively common after events such as a stroke, a head injury or in ongoing neurological conditions. One of the tasks that the frontal lobes of the brain has is to 'inhibit' our behaviour, that is, to 'put the brakes on' something we might be about to do. In the normal course of events, we all think a lot of things but don't say them out loud, which is very good for world peace and getting on well with people we meet, and being tactful. That's down to the effects of the frontal lobes 'putting the social brakes on', and inhibiting our behaviour so that we don't always 'speak our mind'. Similarly we may find ourselves saying things but not acting on them, for example saying 'I feel like punching him', but not actually doing it. This is also possible because our frontal lobes have put the brakes on and inhibited our behaviour.

If the front parts of the brain aren't working as efficiently as they can, it follows then that the social brakes can become less efficient, and people can become what is often called 'dis-inhibited'. This covers a whole range of observations, including people saying some unexpected swear words in the early days after a stroke, people being less tactful than they used to be, and sometimes people becoming aggressive or sexually inappropriate. As with the previous example it is important to acknowledge that there can be other reasons contributing to this kind of behaviour, including pain, discomfort and frustration, all of which can bring anyone closer to the point at which they lose their temper, for example. If there are specific things that can be identified as triggers for strong reactions, then a good starting point is to see if they can be modified.

Secondly, as with the initiation, it can be helpful to arrive at an agreed plan of how to indicate that disinhibition may be having an impact on a conversation without it necessarily being blaming. This requires an agreed plan negotiated in advance that both parties are happy with, and can be as explicit as identifying that this is not how the person would normally choose to act, and suggesting a simple way to try and reduce tension, such as taking a couple of deep breaths. If there are particular situations or people that serve as triggers for disinhibited behaviours and these can't be avoided, then deciding on some ground-rules between you in advance and then reminding each other of the rules during the situation can be a way of dealing with it explicitly but also quite subtly. In some situations it will make life simpler to explain the nature of the difficulties that are being experienced to other people to try and avoid them drawing unwarranted conclusions.

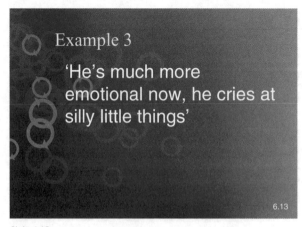

Example 3

'He's much more emotional now, he cries at silly little things'

6.13

Slide 6.13

This example is from the wife of someone who had had a stroke, and she said that 'he's much more emotional now, he cries at silly little things'.

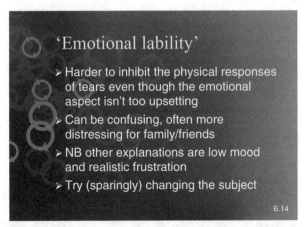

'Emotional lability'
➤ Harder to inhibit the physical responses of tears even though the emotional aspect isn't too upsetting
➤ Can be confusing, often more distressing for family/friends
➤ NB other explanations are low mood and realistic frustration
➤ Try (sparingly) changing the subject

6.14

Slide 6.14

It's not uncommon for people to find themselves crying much more easily when they have had a stroke or a head injury, or in the presence of another neurological condition. It's as if the emotions are lying just underneath the surface and are displayed at the slightest occurrence. It's common enough that it's been given a special name, which is 'emotional lability'. Another term that sometimes is used to describe it is 'emotional incontinence', and although that's not a pleasant phrase it does give the idea of the reduced control that people sometimes have over their displays of emotion. It's usually the case that people find they cry much more easily, although more rarely it's the other extreme and people can find themselves laughing at the slightest thing.

Commonly people will be surprised to find themselves crying over things that wouldn't normally make them cry, for example something they see on the television, or some interaction with another person. It can be very confusing for the individual concerned, as very often they won't be experiencing the emotion of distress but will just be displaying the physical reaction of tears. Often it's more distressing for the people around the person who's crying, as they might think that they have done something to upset that person. The reason for this pattern of crying without necessarily feeling very upset can be thought of as relating to a disconnection between the part of the brain that deals with experiencing emotions and the part of the brain that deals with displaying them. It can also help to think of it as similar to the 'disinhibition' that we mentioned, as it's harder to inhibit the physical response of tears.

As with all the other aspects of behaviour we've mentioned so far, we need to consider some alternative explanations that may also be playing a part. We can't ignore the fact that dealing with the consequences of a brain injury can be realistically distressing and frustrating, and so increased tearfulness can be an entirely natural reaction to the new situation.

In terms of managing emotional lability, it can sometimes be useful to change the subject. In the case of emotional lability, the tears will tend to subside as the topic is changed, which is often not the case when the tears truly do reflect internal distress. While this can be a useful way to distinguish between lability and distress, it is important not to do this too much as constantly changing the subject will mean that it becomes more difficult to have a meaningful conversation.

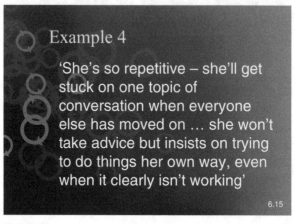

Slide 6.15

The next example is from a man who was describing a change in the way his wife had been acting since her neurological condition became apparent. He says 'she's so repetitive, she'll get stuck on one topic of conversation when everyone else has moved on . . . she won't take advice but insists on trying to do things her own way, even when it clearly isn't working'.

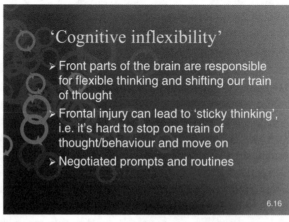

Slide 6.16

One explanation for overly repetitive behaviours or difficulties with moving on from one task or topic to another relates once more to the functions of the frontal lobes. These parts of the brain are involved in flexible thinking and in letting us shift our train of thought from one consideration to the next. If the frontal lobes are injured for some reason, then it can be harder to stop one train of thought or one action that is being carried out and move on to engage with another. It can seem as if someone is 'stuck' on a particular idea or activity and can find it hard to 'unstick' themselves. This difficulty with flexible, adaptable thinking is sometimes described as 'sticky thinking', as it can be hard to keep up with the changing demands of a situation. A common example in the early days after something like a stroke is for someone to be washing themselves and become stuck on washing one arm for example, and then need someone to prompt them to move on to washing the next part of the body.

We began describing executive skills in terms of planning, which included recognising difficulties and thinking flexibly to solve them. One situation that can arise with these sorts of difficulties is that someone may notice that there is a problem and try and solve it in one way, but be unable to generate other ideas to solve the problem if that approach doesn't work. For example, if the kettle isn't boiling, then a good first solution would be to make sure that the 'on' button has been pushed in. However, if on checking that it definitely has been on then the frontal lobes would normally shift away from that potential solution and perhaps check that it is plugged in. If there is some degree of 'sticky thinking' present then someone might become stuck on the first solution, checking that the button is pushed in. The impact of this sort of problem can be very marked as it can make it extremely hard to deal with unexpected problems that are out of the normal routine and may require a few attempts to work out.

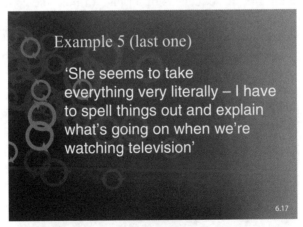

Slide 6.17

The last example is from a man who says that now his wife 'seems to take everything very literally – I have to spell things out and explain what's going on when we're watching television'. Once again the frontal lobes of the brain can be responsible for difficulties such as these.

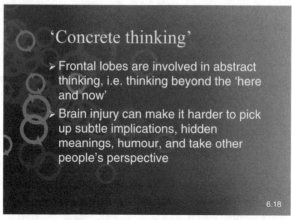

Slide 6.18

The frontal lobes are involved in the ability to think abstractly, that is, to consider things that are beyond the 'here and now'. If there is any injury to the frontal lobes then people can struggle to deal with concepts that aren't concrete, practical and easy to grasp. This would include subtle implications of a television drama's plot, for example if something isn't spelled out but just hinted at. It might also lead to a difficulty with picking up on hidden meanings, for example in the use of humour or sarcasm. It can be hard for people to take other people's perspectives, as this requires the ability to imagine yourself in someone else's position. The analogy of a chief executive of a company can be helpful again, as they would be considering the subtle implications of all the business dealings, and would be imagining the consequences of a range of possible courses of action. The skill of thinking abstractly would be very important to them. If people struggle with this then it can mean that they miss out on some subtleties in everyday interactions and can find it hard to think beyond things that are actually happening at the time.

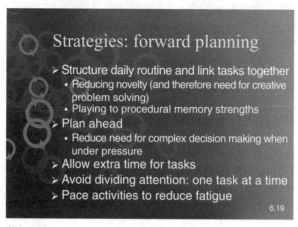

Slide 6.19

There are a number of broad principles that can be applied in order to try and reduce some of the impact of difficulties related to executive function difficulties. One very helpful approach is to try and develop consistent routines or habits where this is practical (Callahan, 2001). By their nature, difficulties with executive skills become particularly apparent in novel, unfamiliar situations, while well-rehearsed, routine tasks can be less affected. The implication of this is that establishing routines and habits can reduce the need to 'problem-solve' situations each time they arise. In certain situations sticking to a consistent procedure can reduce the effort required. Examples might include developing a routine sequence of tasks to go through before leaving the house, or a standard routine of tasks to do when arriving at work, such as checking your diary, checking your post, listening to the answering machine then checking your emails. Not only does sticking to a set routine reduce the need to work out what to do next afresh each time, it also plays to a common strength that people have. Even when there may be difficulties with planning and remembering things, a particular aspect of memory called 'procedural' memory often stays intact, which means that it remains possible to remember and carry out established habits. Of course, there is a balance to be struck between playing to your strengths by establishing routine sets of actions and quality of life; if the whole of every day were to become set into a routine then it might be very boring. However, for certain sets of tasks during the day, establishing a habit can increase the quality of life by increasing the chances of the tasks being achieved. For example, if there is regular medication to be taken at a particular time of day, consistently linking it together with another task can make it more likely to happen (Callahan, 2001), for example always taking the medication with a meal (unless this is not how it is meant to be taken).

When complex decision making is more difficult for someone, then it can become particularly noticeable when there are many demands at the same time and a limited amount of time available to spend weighing up the options and deciding what to do. If you know that there is a decision to make at some point in the near future, try and explicitly plan the day so that you will not have to make the difficult decision in a rush or when there are other demands on you, or when you know that you are likely to be tired (Callahan, 2001). For example, in a work setting, don't leave a big complex task until the end of the day when you will be tired and in a rush. At home, try and arrange in advance what you need to take with you when you go out so that you do not have to make decisions when you are in a rush to leave the house. Plan journeys on public transport in advance, finding out where you need to be when. This will mean that you can write the information down and have it to refer to, rather than having to work it out when you are in a rush and maybe in a crowded distracting place. As complex tasks may be more effortful, they are likely to take longer and so that needs to be allowed for when planning the day. It is important to be realistic about what you will be able to achieve in a set amount of time, as otherwise you can place an extra burden on yourself.

Many of the strategies aimed at minimising the effects of difficulties with attention can be relevant in managing executive difficulties, as 'divided attention' is a matter of allocating resources, prioritising what's going on around you and monitoring a complex situation. Reducing distractions is a basic step, but it is also useful to plan the day such that, wherever possible, you only have one task to focus on at any one time.

Of relevance to planning the day ahead, as it is extremely common for people to experience marked fatigue, it is also helpful to schedule in regular rest periods during activities. This often means that you will be able to achieve more during the day than if you persevere with a task to the point of exhaustion.

Organising the day into routines where possible and structuring the activities that you need to do so that they can be tackled one at a time takes some executive skills in itself. It can therefore be helpful to involve someone else with this planning stage to make sure that the plan itself is practical. Although some people do not like the idea of relying on someone else for help in this manner, working together at this stage with someone you trust (be that a family member, friend or work colleague) in planning the day ahead can mean that you will be able to act more independently and successfully while carrying out the tasks themselves. This introduces the idea of being prompted.

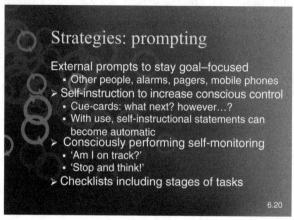

Slide 6.20

Executive function difficulties often mean that there is the need for some sort of external prompt to raise awareness that a difficulty has arisen, and subsequently to implement a solution. Such a prompt can come from another person, but some people prefer inanimate prompting, such as might be achieved by using alarms with verbal statements attached, as this can reduce the feelings of reliance on another person and increase the feelings of independence. People can make use of a range of devices to prompt themselves, including the hourly chime on a digital watch, alarms on mobile phones, electronic personal organisers or paging systems.

Sometimes it is possible to mimic consciously the 'self-monitoring' task of the brain by establishing a habit of asking yourself to review the current situation. A standard set phrase along the lines of 'am I on track?' or 'stop and think' can act as a prompt to make sure that the overall goal is being achieved. It can be helpful to have such a statement written out somewhere where it will catch your eye, for example on the desk at work, or in the kitchen, or stuck onto your watch strap so that you will see it when the hourly chime goes off. Some people find it helpful to write out such statements on 'cue cards' to keep in their wallet or purse such that they have a prompt to help them if they do find themselves in a complex situation requiring decision making. Other people are able to learn the phrase such that they can repeat it to themselves when faced with complex tasks.

Subtle prompts to carry out this deliberate 'self-monitoring' can be placed in the environment in which they will be most relevant, for example coloured dots stuck on the wall which will serve as reminders to 'stop and think' but not mean anything to other people. This approach of using external prompts can be helpful with staying on track with the task in hand, and also means that you will be reminded to consider the consequences of the action currently being performed, thus reducing the chances of acting without doing so. Similarly, they can be helpful if there is a difficulty with initiation of actions. External prompts can also be helpful in managing situations in which someone may be 'stuck' on a particular stage of a task; a noticeable prompt combined with a 'self-talk statement' of 'what should I be doing now?' can help with moving onto the next stage towards achieving the overall goal. For tasks with many stages, use of a checklist can also be combined with a prompt and self-talk to keep on track.

The more of a habit using such 'self-talk' becomes, the less need there may be to rely on external prompts to bring them to mind during the course of the day. All these suggestions relating to planning ahead and being prompted by some means are not serving to 'cure' any difficulties with executive function, but are aiming to compensate for any existing inefficiencies by deliberately and consciously mimicking those mental processes that would normally be going on without any conscious effort.

Difficulties with executive function can make it easier to become distracted from the overall goal, particularly when there are many stages involved in achieving that goal. This can lead to the situation where much activity results in little progress. One approach that can help with keeping the overall goal in mind, and hence help with keeping tabs on whether it is being achieved or not, is called the 'mental blackboard' technique (Evans, 2002a).

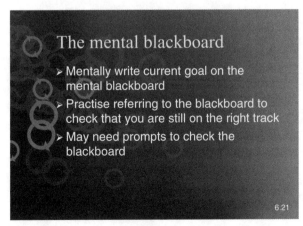

Slide 6.21

The strategy involved with this is to use your imagination to 'write' on an imaginary blackboard what it is you need to achieve. Some people find it easier to use images rather than words, in which case imagining drawing a mental representation of the goal on the blackboard is the strategy to adopt. It is important to imagine that the images or words are written very clearly on the board, and that they represent the main task very clearly. The mental blackboard needs to be checked regularly, and alarms or other reminders can be a useful way to prompt this, as can simple 'self-talk' statements, such as 'what am I aiming for?' Before starting any task, make sure that the goal is clearly imagined on your mental blackboard, and during the task make sure you keep checking the blackboard to increase the chances of staying on track. Once the task is finished, imagine wiping the blackboard clean (Evans, 2002a).

The first stage in solving any problem that may arise in either the home or the works setting is to notice that the problem is there in the first place. While combining reminder systems with statements such as 'stop and think' or 'take stock''may help to encourage deliberate consideration of the presence of anything that needs to be addressed, it can remain the case that it can be hard to appreciate when things might be harder than before the difficulties arose. There are often benefits to enlisting the help of, for example, a trusted colleague. It's important that it's someone from whom you are prepared to hear feedback about your performance, as it can be a very sensitive matter. You have to be prepared to give them permission to give you honest feedback, which may involve saying things you may not want to hear, for example stating if you are less organised or less tactful than before any of the difficulties arose. Having identified if there are any changes, then you and those supporting you are better placed to implement some of the strategies we have mentioned to address them.

Even when noticing problems is not any harder then usual, it can be effortful to make decisions about the best way to tackle them. It can sometimes be helpful to break down the process of making a decision about how to solve a problem into a series of questions (Evans, 2001).

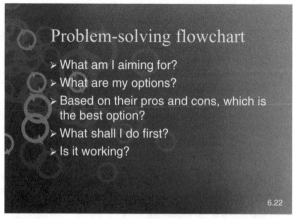

Slide 6.22

As with the brief 'self-talk' statements, it can be helpful to write down a problem-solving flowchart like this on a card, which can be kept in a wallet or handbag to help deal with unexpected situations. Using this approach consciously mimics the usual mental processes we take for granted, and can be rehearsed using made-up examples or stories taken from the news (Evans, 2001).

Mentally working through a decision-making flowchart, or if it helps, writing out the stages of the flowchart, can make it more likely that the decision arrived at is based on consideration of the consequences and the advantages/disadvantages. This approach takes practice to be effective, but consideration of even one stage of the flowchart (for example 'what are my choices here?') may serve as a prompt that will aid effective decision making.

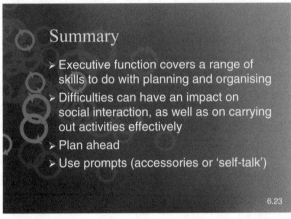

Slide 6.23

In summary, there are a range of skills related to executive function, including planning and organising skills, which can have subtle but noticeable effects in home, work and social settings. People being aware of any such difficulties is important in avoiding misinterpretation and also in keeping realistic expectations. Planning ahead, often with the help of other people, can help to avoid some difficulties, as can using prompts of various sorts to try and keep on track and help with decision making.

Executive Function

While some functions of the brain, such as memory or concentration, seem obvious to us, 'executive function' is usually less familiar. The term 'executive' describes well the range of tasks that this group of skills (usually associated with the front parts of the brain) cover, as they are similar to the roles that the chief executive of a company would fulfil. They can be summarised as:

- Planning: deciding on the best plan of action.
- Implementing: putting the plan into practice.
- Monitoring: keeping track of whether the plan is being effective and considering changes if it is not.

For example, in a work setting, someone may have to consider a range of tasks that needs to be carried out, and make judgements about which ones are the most important and which ones need to be completed first in order to meet deadlines. This would result in a plan of action being formed. Then, this plan would need to be put into action, and, while the plan is being carried out, the person would need to keep checking that they were on track towards achieving all the targets. If the plan is not being effective they would need to recognise that and alter the plan accordingly, possibly changing the priorities.

Difficulties with 'executive function' can make some or all of these skills more difficult. It doesn't mean that someone has become less intelligent, but they can find it much more effortful to deal with multiple demands, put plans into action, recognise problems and think flexibly.

Practical management of executive difficulties

1. Difficulties with executive skills become particularly apparent in novel, unfamiliar situations, while well-rehearsed, routine tasks can be less affected. The implication of this is that establishing routines and habits can reduce the need to 'problem-solve' situations each time they arise. In certain situations sticking to a consistent procedure can reduce the effort required (e.g. having a routine sequence of tasks to go through before leaving the house, or a routine sequence for elements of work such as checking the diary, post, answering machine and emails.)
2. Clearly there are many situations in daily life that cannot easily have the structure of a routine imposed on them. In these circumstances, it can be helpful to attempt to mimic consciously the elements of decision making that we would normally go through without much conscious effort. Mentally working through a decision-making

flowchart, or if it helps, writing out the stages of the flowchart, can make it more likely that the decision arrived at is based on consideration of the consequences and the advantages/disadvantages. Such a flowchart might include some or all of the following stages:

What am I aiming for?

↓

What are my options?

↓

Based on their pros and cons, which is the best option?

↓

What shall I do first?

↓

Is it working?

3. Try experimenting with the sort of checklist above; it may be that even making a deliberate effort to consider one of the stages is helpful, and some people find it helpful to have phrases that they say to themselves when faced with a problem they have to solve, such as 'what are my choices?', 'am I on track?', or more general statements such as 'stop and think'. Some people find it helpful to write down such statements and have them on cards in places that that they will see, for example on their desk at work.

4. One particular situation that can cause difficulties arises when a task has many stages to it that need to be kept in mind and carried out in a particular order, such as cooking a meal. Writing out a checklist can be a useful way of imposing structure on a situation such as this, which has the potential to become overwhelming, as several different tasks need to be coordinated. Preparing a checklist of the different stages and combining this with a stock statement, such as 'stop and think', can be effective.

5. One aspect of executive difficulties relates to implementing plans, that is turning intention into action. It can be helpful to make use of prompts, such as alarms on watches, mobile phones or computers, or reminders from other people, to reduce the likelihood of intentions not being carried out.

6. It can sometimes be easier to become distracted from the overall goal, particularly when there are many stages towards achieving it, with the result that much activity results in little progress. One suggestion to help keep the overall goal in mind, which will help with keeping tabs on whether it is being achieved or not, is to try something that has been called the 'mental blackboard'. The trick is to use your imagination to 'write' on the imaginary blackboard what it is you need to achieve. Some people will find it easier to use images rather than words. It is important to imagine that the image/words are written very clearly on the board,

and that they represent the main task very clearly. It is important to check your mental blackboard regularly, and alarms or other reminders can be a useful way to prompt this; simple statements to yourself can also help, for example 'what am I aiming for?'. Before starting a task make sure that the goal is clearly imagined on your mental backboard, and during the task make sure you keep checking the blackboard to increase the chances of staying on track. Once the task is finished, imagine wiping the blackboard clean.

7. As 'divided attention' tasks (i.e. trying to do more than one thing at once) require some of the skills related to executive function, the general advice is to try and structure activities such that you are only attempting one thing at any one time, and minimise distractions by working in a quiet environment.

As by its nature executive function includes being aware of difficulties, it can be the case that people who struggle with some of these skills find it very difficult to acknowledge that they are having any such difficulties. This can be easily misinterpreted as stubbornness or non-cooperation, but is better thought of as a feature of the condition. By its nature, if this is the case then it can be very difficult for people to implement any of the strategies independently and help from supportive others is often required.

Things to consider

- In what settings do you struggle to keep on track with the task? Work? Cooking? Conversations? Is there any one you trust to give you honest objective feedback about this?
- How can you reduce distractions in these settings? How can you plan tasks so you have only one thing at a time to work on? Can you enlist any help with this, for example from colleagues or family members?
- What can you incorporate into a routine that can stay consistent each time, to reduce the novelty on each occasion? Practise this in each setting in which it can be relevant.
- Are there any statements/phrases that you can have as prompts for yourself to see if you are staying on track with what you are hoping to achieve? If someone else is going to prompt you, what phrase are you both happy to be used so that it won't feel like nagging?
- What else can you use to prompt yourself to check that you are monitoring your progress with a task? Alarms, mobile phone, personal computer?
- Can you use a checklist to help you through more complicated, multi-stage tasks?
- Experiment with using a 'mental blackboard' to keep tabs on your overall goal.

Chapter 7
Thoughts and Feelings

Comments about material

The material in this chapter adopts an explicitly cognitive-behavioural therapy (CBT) approach. While other psychotherapeutic models clearly have their merits, the CBT approach is, in general, the one with the most convincing evidence base (Roth & Fonagy, 1996). Its more concrete approach lends itself to being tailored to client groups who may find more abstract concepts and interpretations harder to deal with due to cognitive limitations (Gracey, 2002).

The CBT approach has also been used extensively in interventions with chronic health-related conditions with its focus on intervention at the level of the appraisals that people make of their situations (Moorey, 1996), and it is able to accommodate the reality of the distressing situation in which people with brain injury find themselves. The CBT approach lends itself to simple explanation, which has the dual advantage of rendering it explicable to people with some degree of cognitive impairment, and also rendering it more acceptable as a way of intervening with people who by no means have a 'mental health' problem and may be resistant to psychological approaches.

There is much to be gained from other psychotherapeutic approaches however, and some of their tenets are extremely useful to bear in mind in rehabilitation interventions, without necessarily being stated explicitly. Processes such as externalising and normalising are inherent in much intervention (both group-based and individual), and are strongly identified with a narrative approach (White & Epston, 1990). Bion's (1970) characterisation of the therapist as a 'container' can be an extremely useful model, particularly when attempting to manage anxiety within a multidisciplinary team. In considering one's own reactions to the often tragic context in which people are engaging in rehabilitation, notions of transference and countertransference can be of some utility (Heiman, 1950), while increasingly the impact of a brain injury upon a person's family and loved ones is being acknowledged and hence consideration of some systemic principles can inform intervention (Maitz & Sachs, 1995).

It remains the case, however, that the content of the session presented here is unashamedly cognitive-behavioural in nature. A number of authors advocate its use with people who have experienced a brain injury (e.g. Fleminger, Oliver, Williams & Evans, 2003), while Khan-Bourne and Brown (2003) describe the promising nature of research evaluating the use of CBT after brain injury.

While it is apparent that the shared experience of attendees is likely to be far more powerful than a didactic 'facts about emotional responses to brain injury' presentation by a health professional, the session begins somewhat in this latter vein. This is done with intent to normalise. If a description of some of the more common emotional responses to a brain injury can engender a response of 'it's not just me then', then this can help in reducing one element of emotional burden in what is likely to be a stressful situation for many reasons.

Material to include

Slide 7.1

This session is somewhat different in its content to the other sessions. Most of the other sessions have focused on specific skills that the brain is involved in, such as remembering things or concentrating. In this session, we'll be considering people's emotional responses to the situation in which they find themselves. For some people that can be a real turn-off, and they feel quite able to cope without struggling with feelings of, for example, hopelessness or helplessness. Those people can rest assured that this session is fairly practical in nature. The way that we'll suggest dealing with distress is applicable to anyone at all in the general population, brain injury or not, so it may well still be of some relevance and interest for you either now or at some point in the future. For other people, the emotional side of things has an enormous impact on their daily lives. For example, a loss of confidence or worrying about what other people might think can mean that people stop themselves doing some activities that they'd like to.

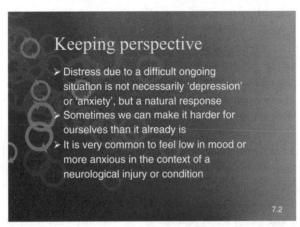

Slide 7.2

Before we start to think about managing distress, there are a couple of broad points that it's worth making. The first is that what we'll be considering doesn't mean we're talking about clinically defined diagnoses of 'depression' or 'anxiety'. We know that, for reasons that are perhaps obvious, reactions such as depression are quite common after something like a stroke or a head injury, or in an ongoing neurological condition, but we need to recognise that for most people there is going to be a natural reaction to a realistically distressing health-related event. Common sense tells us that that will usually be the case, and often there isn't a great need to 'psychologise' what is an entirely appropriate response to an unexpected and unpleasant change. There's something to be said for not interfering with people's own coping strategies, which can often be very effective (NICE, 2005). Sometimes though, people can find themselves making the situation even more distressing for themselves than it already is, and that's what we're going to focus on. We can't wave a magic wand and pretend everything's exactly how we'd want it to be, and we can't lose sight of the fact that that means there's a level of distress that is to be expected, but we can try and stop the distress levels being any higher than they need to be.

The second thing to acknowledge is that it's very common to struggle with feeling low in mood, or to feel more anxiety or irritability when you're living with the consequences of some injury to the brain. Here are a handful of very common worries that people report:

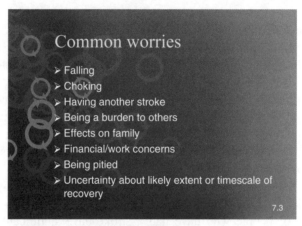

Slide 7.3

It's clear that most of these may have an element of realism to them. For example, after a stroke, or during a bad spell with multiple sclerosis, then it really is more difficult to keep your balance on uneven pavements, and so there may be an increased risk of falling. It may well be the case that it is harder to swallow food than it was before, and so there is an increased risk of choking.

For many people there is uncertainty about the expected course of their condition, and uncertainty about what recovery will occur and over what timescale. If somebody has had a stroke there can be a big fear of having another stroke. There can be fear relating to having another relapse of an ongoing condition. There can also be a whole range of practical concerns that can cause great anxiety, including worries about the effects of a condition on family members, and financial concerns relating to work, housing and benefits.

It may be that some of these concerns seem very relevant, or there may be others that you're aware are more worrying for you in your particular situation. Whatever the particular worries may be for you, the message to take from this is that you're not alone in having concerns such as these.

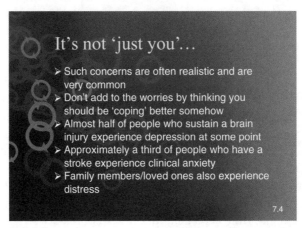

Slide 7.4

Sometimes people can find themselves worrying about factors such as the ones we've listed, and then can worry about their worrying, saying to themselves 'I'm sure other people in my situation wouldn't be getting in such a state – I'm really not coping well at all, I'm not as strong in this situation as I thought I might be'. That kind of thinking is one way in which people can make a difficult situation even more distressing than it genuinely is. One reason for mentioning some of these difficulties is to try and make the point that this kind of situation is difficult. People have every right to be finding it hard, and many many people do find it very hard. If one concern you have is 'I'm not coping as well as I should' then it's important for you to recognise that it isn't just you that finds this tough. A couple of statistics to back that up are that about half of people who experience a brain injury will meet the criteria for depression at some stage (Fleminger et al., 2003). Estimates vary, but anything up to about a third of people who have had a stroke have significant levels of anxiety (Gillespie, 1997). Anxiety often goes along with depression, and we know that realistic difficulties play a part in anxiety, for example difficulty swallowing can lead to worry about choking, and difficulty with balance can lead to worry about falling (Astrom, 1996).

This information is not intended to concern you if you're feeling that you're coping well at the moment, but rather to make the point that it is very common to feel anxious or low in mood. It's certainly nothing to feel ashamed or weak about, anymore than you would about any of the other consequences of an injury to the brain, for example weakness in a limb. It's important for us to acknowledge that people close to the person with the acquired brain injury or neurological condition can struggle with strong negative emotions too, including guilt and their own responses to any changes that have been forced on the nature of their relationships.

Having acknowledged the fact that it is very common to struggle with managing the emotional consequences of living with a brain injury or neurological condition, we need to consider practical ways to manage such distress. This is a useful way of thinking about any upsetting situation that you find yourself in:

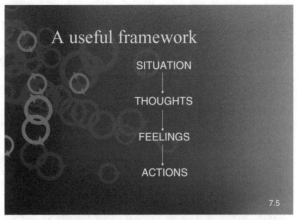

Slide 7.5

Let's work through an example (after Beck, 1976). Imagine that the situation you find yourself in is that you are asleep in bed at night and you hear a crash downstairs. You may think 'it's a burglar', in which case you may feel scared and take the action of hiding. In the same situation, if you are asleep in bed at night and hear a crash, you may alternatively think 'that's a member of my family coming home late'. You may then feel relieved, and get up to greet them. If you were to hear a crash in the night and think 'I left a window open and the draught has blown a vase over', you may feel irritated, but just go back to sleep.

The point of that example is to demonstrate that exactly the same situation (hearing a crash) can lead to very different feelings (scared, relieved or irritated) and different actions. That doesn't make sense unless you consider the 'thoughts' stage from the flowchart. Our appraisal of the situation plays a big part in our reaction to it.

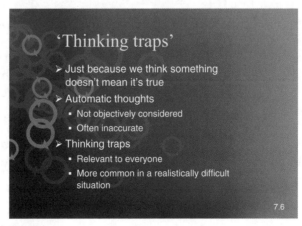

Slide 7.6

Just because we think something doesn't necessarily mean that it is true or accurate. Some of the thoughts we have are often called 'automatic thoughts' because they just pop into our heads without being carefully considered. Often they are not accurate, and if that's the case then we're in danger of falling into 'thinking traps'. In day-to-day life, we all fall into 'thinking traps' that make us feel more distressed than we need to. These 'thinking traps' are easier to fall into when we find ourselves in a realistically difficult situation, such as dealing with the consequences of some sort of injury to the brain.

To give an example of a couple of thinking traps, let's consider someone playing football who makes a mistake which leads to the other side scoring. It may be that they instantly think to themselves 'oh no, I'm rubbish at this game; the other lads will never speak to me again'. Straight away that person has fallen into two very common thinking traps. The first is often called 'all or nothing' thinking.

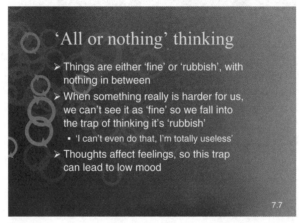

Slide 7.7

This is the trap of assuming that everything is either 'fine' or it's 'rubbish', with nothing in between. The danger here is that as soon as anything happens that makes it apparent that the situation can't be appraised as being 100% 'fine', the trap springs into action and we can end up thinking to ourselves that everything is 100% 'rubbish'. This can be extremely relevant for people when they are finding some things more difficult due to a brain injury or a neurological condition.

If we find something more difficult than we'd hoped, or we don't do something as well as we would want to, it is easy to fall into the trap of thinking 'I'm no good at that, I'm totally useless'. We saw above that what we think affects how we feel and it's obvious that if we think 'I'm useless' then we're going to feel down.

Often, when we are able to stop and think objectively about our situation, we discover that it isn't accurate to conclude that 'I'm totally useless'. When living with a brain injury or neurological condition it's often more accurate to conclude something like 'at the moment some things are harder for me than before, but there are some things at which I'm just as good as ever'.

For example, in a situation in which it is harder to speak the words that you want to, an automatic thought might be 'I can't even make myself understood, I'm no good to anyone'. This kind of thought can be particularly distressing for a person who has always been very independent and had responsibilities that they currently can't carry out.

We've seen that what we think affects how we feel, so the all-or-nothing thinking trap, which means that if something isn't as good as we think it 'should' be we conclude that it's totally useless, commonly makes people feel quite depressed.

The second trap, which the footballer fell into, was to think 'the lads will never speak to me again'. He was imagining the worst-case scenario.

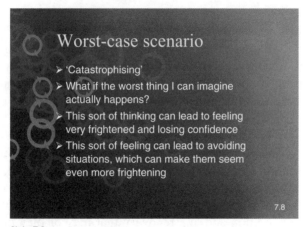

Slide 7.8

This is another common thinking trap that arises when people are trying to cope with an ongoing difficulty. The name given to the trap of imagining the worst that could happen is 'catastrophisation', and anything with a name like that can't be a good thing. For example, the 'situation' in our flowchart might be that it is harder to keep your balance when walking to the shops. The danger is that the 'thoughts' stage consists of a catastrophisation thinking trap along the lines of 'I'll fall over and hit my head, and that'll make everything worse, and I might die and that'll upset my family'. It's apparent that if that is the 'thoughts' stage of the flowchart then the 'feelings' stage will be something akin to 'terrified', and the 'action' stage might be to avoid putting yourself in that situation, maybe by not leaving the house.

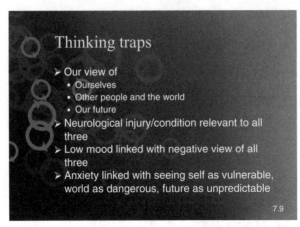

Slide 7.9

The thinking traps can often relate to our view of our ourselves, our view of other people and the world generally, and our view of the future (Beck, 1967, cited in Moorey, 1996). It's easy to see how our view of all three aspects can be affected by a neurological condition. Our view of ourselves as independent people in control of our lives can take a knock if some physical or mental tasks have become harder for us, with the result that we find ourselves having to be more reliant on other people than we'd choose to be. Our view of the world and other people can easily become altered if we fall into the trap of thinking that we know what other people are thinking. For example, it's easy to find yourself assuming that other people are thinking that you're stupid if it's harder to get the words out as quickly as you're used to, or assuming that they think you can't do anything for yourself if you're needing to use a wheelchair. For many people, there is a degree of uncertainty about what the future holds in terms of the course of the condition and any recovery that may or may not be expected. A thinking trap would be to think that 'nothing will ever be good for me again'. If someone has a negative view of all three aspects (themselves, other people and the future), then there's a good chance that their mood will be low, and they may be feeling depressed.

If people are feeling anxious, there's often a combination of seeing yourself as more vulnerable, seeing the world as more dangerous, and seeing the future as unpredictable (Blackburn & Davidson, 1990, cited in Moorey, 1996). For many people, there is some realistic foundation for some of these appraisals, but there is the danger of falling into thinking traps and appraising the situation as being even worse than it realistically is.

Having introduced the idea of thinking traps that can make us feel worse than we need to, we can start to think about how to manage them. There are essentially two stages to combating the thinking traps. First, we need to identify the negative automatic thoughts, and second, we need to challenge them.

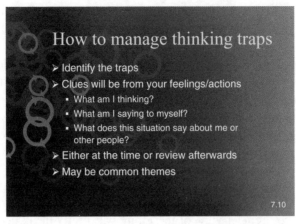

How to manage thinking traps

➤ Identify the traps
➤ Clues will be from your feelings/actions
  ▪ What am I thinking?
  ▪ What am I saying to myself?
  ▪ What does this situation say about me or other people?
➤ Either at the time or review afterwards
➤ May be common themes

7.10

Slide 7.10

Identifying the thinking traps isn't always easy. The clue to spotting when we may be falling into one comes from how we're feeling or acting. The flowchart on which we're basing this approach would suggest that if we're falling into an unrealistic appraisal of the situation, then we're likely to be feeling strong emotions, for example feeling very down, worried or angry. That in turn can lead on to actions such as avoiding situations or acting in an irritable way. When you do find yourself feeling strong emotions or acting in untoward ways, that's the time to try and consider what your appraisal of the current situation is. Ask yourself questions like these:

❑ What is going through my mind?
❑ What am I saying to myself?
❑ What does this situation say about me, the world, other people or the future?

Sometimes by the very nature of the feelings, it can be hard to stop and consider what you're thinking at that very moment. Sometimes it can be easier to take a few minutes at the end of the day when things might be a bit calmer to reflect on the circumstances you've found frustrating or distressing. Often there will be a theme for people, that is, a particular thinking trap that is triggered by a range of situations. Identifying which trap or traps are most common for you is a good first step to managing distress.

Consider this example to try and make the theory a bit more relevant to day-to-day life. A lady had a stroke four months ago and she's made quite a good recovery. She still has little movement in her right arm though, and it is hard for her to find all the words that she wants. She still has some slurred speech and she finds it more difficult to remember things that people have told her, so she struggles to remember people's names and to keep up with conversations. This is making it harder for her to take part in some of her leisure activities, such as looking after her grandchildren and going for a drink with friends. In particular, she finds it very embarrassing when she has to order drinks from the bar, as she finds it hard to remember what drinks people wanted, and also it can be difficult to make herself understood when she is asking for them. As a result she has started to avoid going out with her friends because she was starting to feel self-conscious.

She'd always been very involved with helping other people out by doing charity work, but now her fatigue levels mean she isn't able to do so much. She's had to say 'no' to some things, which she would never have done before her stroke.

This lady was very critical of herself, and she saw the fact that she wasn't able to do all the things she used to do as a failure on her part. She also saw the fact that she wasn't able to do some things as accurately as before as a failure on her part. She began to see herself as completely useless. She began to assume that other people would be thinking that she was useless too, and she worried that other people would think she'd become lazy or disinterested because she wasn't carrying out the same levels of activity as before. Her view of the future was pretty bleak because she couldn't see how things were going to change. She thought that she should be able to carry on just as before with all the roles that she had in life, and if she couldn't then she was letting people down.

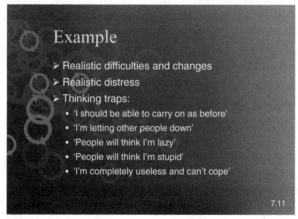

Slide 7.11

Overall, this is a realistically distressing situation in which a stroke has made many of this lady's usual activities more difficult or even impossible at present. That is the objective appraisal of the situation, which is accurate and can't be ignored. Just 'thinking positively' and trying to ignore the difficulties may work to an extent, but is unlikely to be a useful long-term strategy because there are likely to be daily reminders of the reality that some things are more difficult now. That realistic appraisal of the situation is of course going to be associated with some sadness and distress, as we saw from the flow-chart earlier, that suggests that what we think affects how we feel. However, this lady then fell into some thinking traps. She was thinking 'I should be able to carry on as before', and 'I mustn't let other people down'. She was thinking 'people will think

I'm lazy' when she couldn't do something because of her arm or her fatigue. When she was out with friends she was imposing the expectation on herself that 'I must get the words exactly right or other people will think I'm stupid'. When she couldn't meet her own demands on herself she fell into more thinking traps that were complete overgeneralisations, such as 'I'm a failure', 'I'm completely useless' and 'I can't cope with this situation'.

Taking it back to our flowchart, we can see that these thinking traps are going to make this lady feel worse than she does already. They may make the difference between feeling quite unhappy and feeling very depressed and wondering if it's worthwhile carrying on.

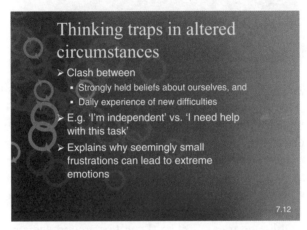

Slide 7.12

The reason why it is so common for people to fall into thinking traps after a brain injury or if they have a neurological condition relates to a clash between the daily experiences of realistic difficulties and strongly held personal beliefs about ourselves that we develop as we grow up. For many of us, we learn to see ourselves as very independent, and it doesn't come naturally to ask someone else for help, as it can feel like a sign of weakness. That can be a useful belief to hold about ourselves in the normal course of events, and can make people quite self-reliant. However, if our circumstances do change because of something involving the brain, and as a result we can't be so self-reliant, then our daily experiences will clash with our long-held beliefs about being independent and not asking for help. Even if it is a relatively small thing that has become more difficult to do independently, it can be seen as representing a failure, and that doesn't sit well with beliefs about relying on yourself. That is very fertile ground for thinking traps, such as 'I'm completely useless', to spring up.

Once you've identified what the automatic thought is (for example 'I'm no good at anything', 'other people resent me', 'I've let everyone down'), the next stage is to challenge it.

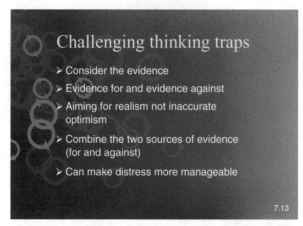

Slide 7.13

If a court of law wants to decide whether something is true or not, then the jury considers the evidence that supports the fact that it is true, and also the evidence that doesn't support it, and then arrives at a balanced decision. That's exactly the approach to take with the negative automatic thoughts that you've identified. Imagine making up a chart with two columns, one for evidence that supports the automatic thought, and one for evidence that doesn't support it. It's important to include both columns because what we're aiming for is a realistic statement, not an inaccurately optimistic one.

For example, if a man who has children were to have had a stroke that made it harder for him to speak, his thinking trap might be 'I can't be a good dad anymore'. That would be an 'all or nothing' thinking trap, in that he's appraising himself as either being a 'good dad' or a 'bad dad' with no gradations in between. The evidence supporting the idea that he can't be a good dad is that he can't talk to his children as well as he could previously. Evidence that doesn't support the idea that he can't be a good dad includes things that he is still able to do, for example hug them, communicate by other means, play with them and love them just as much as ever.

The aim is to arrive at a more realistic appraisal of the situation, and this can be done by combining the evidence for and against the thinking trap. In this case, it might be something along the lines of 'it's harder for me to interact at the moment, but there are still things I can do that mean I'm a good dad to my children'.

The fact that the situation is realistically difficult means that this kind of approach won't magically take away all distress, but making your thoughts more realistic can make the difference between a really bad day and a manageable one. Practising this approach makes it more effective; it can feel somewhat longwinded initially, but once you've been able to identify the common thinking traps that may apply to you regularly, then you can be somewhat 'forearmed' by having more realistic appraisals of the situation prepared in advance with which to challenge the negative automatic thoughts. It can even be helpful to write some realistic statements down, such as 'it's worth trying this even though it might take me longer than it used to'.

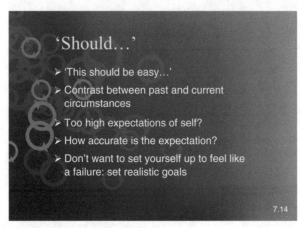

'Should...'
> 'This should be easy...'
> Contrast between past and current circumstances
> Too high expectations of self?
> How accurate is the expectation?
> Don't want to set yourself up to feel like a failure: set realistic goals

7.14

Slide 7.14

A common warning sign that you're falling into a thinking trap is finding yourself using the word 'should' a lot when thinking about yourself and your situation, for example, 'I should be able to do this by myself' or 'this should be easy'. This high-lights the contrast between how things always used to be, and the realistic difficulties that may be part of daily life at present. The level of expectation that we put on our-selves can make us feel as if we're failing if we don't live up to it, with a subsequent impact on how we're feeling. The accuracy of a statement such as 'this should be easy', can be evaluated by examining the evidence. On the one hand, it may be that it is a task such as tying laces that has always been very easy to carry out in the past. On the other hand, in the altered circumstances following a condition involving the brain, evidence that might suggest it isn't an accurate statement could include the fact that now it's harder to move your fingers, and also that perhaps at this stage after the onset of the condition most people wouldn't be expected to be able to carry it out. A more realistic appraisal of the situation, rather than 'this should be easy' would be some-thing like 'although this is usually easy for me, in the current circumstances it is likely to take me longer or I'll need some help with it'. Aiming at a more realistic expecta-tion of yourself in your current circumstances can reduce the number of occasions when you can make yourself feel like a failure for not meeting unrealistic goals.

Once again we need to acknowledge that there will be very appropriate sadness about the realistic fact that some things are harder now, but we need to try to distinguish between that realistic appraisal and some of the thinking traps that are overlaid on that.

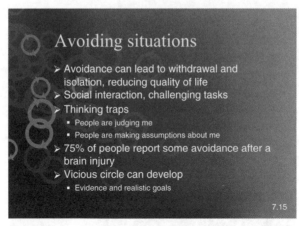

Slide 7.15

One very common 'action' that results from feeling either anxious or low in mood is avoidance of the situations that lead to these feelings. One concern is that if people start to avoid activities that they previously obtained pleasure from, then they can start to be withdrawn and feel even more depressed and isolated. A wide range of situations can make people feel uncomfortable. These include social situations and interactions, and taking on challenging tasks. A range of thinking traps can play a part, such as thinking that other people are judging your performance negatively and making assumptions about you. These situations can occur very frequently, and if the 'thoughts' stage of the flow-chart is that people will be judging you, then the 'feelings' are going to be negative, and the 'action' may well be to avoid that situation. This is a common reaction – about three-quarters of people with acquired brain injury report avoiding at least some situations while about a third of them report a great many instances – ten or more – of avoiding certain situations (Riley, 2005).

Once people start avoiding situations, then a vicious circle can develop whereby the longer you avoid doing something, the harder it becomes to get on and do it. This makes sense when you think about the two columns of evidence that we considered when challenging our thinking traps. For example, if you're worried about falling when walking to the shop and so you don't do it for a few weeks or even months, then the anxiety can escalate because there's been little evidence recently that you are able to do it without coming to harm. Often the most helpful thing to do to bring back self-confidence is to take action such that you start to accumulate evidence that you'll be okay if you try. This might involve actually walking to the shops (or going into the supermarket, or making a phone call, or whatever the specific anxiety relates to), but doing it in a way that it is most likely to succeed, for example being accompanied in the first instance, or allowing yourself extra time, or just buying a few things instead of the whole weekly shopping list. Building up to your goals gradually, rather than setting yourself up to fail by attempting too much at once, is an important part of increasing confidence.

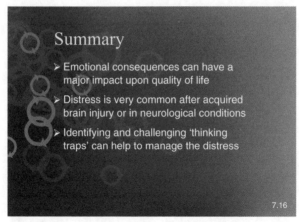

Slide 7.16

In summary, many people find that the emotional consequences of an acquired brain injury or neurological condition have a big impact on their quality of life. This is really quite common and we've discussed some of the reasons why that is the case. We've acknowledged that it can be a realistically distressing situation, and we've also covered a useful framework to help us to manage some of the distress that we can impose on ourselves by falling into 'thinking traps' that make us feel worse than we need to. The good news is that by identifying and challenging our own thinking traps, then we can attempt to reduce the impact that feelings such as frustration, self-consciousness, anxiety and depression can have on daily life.

Thoughts and Feelings

For obvious reasons it is very common for people to feel low in mood when they or their family have to deal with the consequences of a brain injury. It is also common for people to experience more anxieties, and to lose confidence. Many of the common concerns are related to things that may have become realistically more difficult, for example walking, or swallowing, or speaking clearly. Other concerns may relate more to the effects on other people, or to other people's perceptions of us.

Although there are likely to be a number of realistic difficulties, sometimes we can all fall into 'thinking traps' that can make the situation even more distressing for us than it already is. A useful framework for considering our responses to distressing situations is as follows:

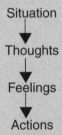

Situation

Thoughts

Feelings

Actions

The same situation can lead to very different feelings depending on what appraisal is made of the situation in the 'thoughts' stage of this flowchart. For example, hearing a noise in the middle of the night may make someone feel scared if they think it's a burglar, or relieved if they think it's a member of their family returning home, or annoyed if they think that it's the cat knocking over a vase. These different feelings will often result in different 'actions', for example hiding, going downstairs, or going back to sleep.

Just because we think something does not mean that it is true. Particularly in very challenging circumstances (such as dealing with the consequences of a brain injury) everyone finds themselves having thoughts that are not objectively accurate, and these then affect how we feel and how we act.

One common example of such a thinking trap is called 'all or nothing' thinking. If we find something harder than we'd like to we may find ourselves thinking 'I can't even do that, I'm totally useless'. Objectively, it usually isn't the case that someone is totally useless; after a brain injury it may be that many things are harder than they used to be but some skills will be just as good as ever. The flowchart above tells us that if we mistakenly appraise a situation as indicating that we are completely useless, then we are likely to feel worse than the situation would objectively deserve.

Another common thinking trap is to imagine the very worst that could happen; if the 'situation' is that it is harder to walk steadily at present, then the thinking trap might be to think that you will fall and hit your head and die; a thought like that will lead to fear of carrying out a task. A likely consequence for the 'actions' stage is avoidance of situations that lead to such thinking traps.

Managing thinking traps: 'identify and challenge'

The first stage in managing such thinking traps is to identify when you may be falling into them. Often this will be when you notice yourself becoming upset or angry. Review such situations and ask yourself what you may have been thinking at the time: What did that situation say about you? What do you think other people might have been thinking about you? It may be the case that there are themes that emerge, in that the same thinking trap underlies different situations that are distressing.

Once the thinking traps have been identified, the next stage is to challenge them. The aim is to arrive at a more realistic appraisal of the situation. This is done by weighing up the evidence as to whether or not the appraisal of the situation is correct. It is important to consider evidence that does support the thinking trap as well as evidence that does not, in order to arrive at a realistic appraisal of the situation. For example:

- *Situation:* I can't do up my shoelaces.
- *Thoughts:* I'm completely useless (subsequent feelings of depression and action of avoiding going outdoors as this requires shoes, adding social isolation to the depression).
- *Evidence for 'being completely useless':* I can't move my fingers at the moment; this means it takes longer to do some things; some things I can't do at all at present.
- *Evidence against 'being completely useless':* I can still do many things that don't need fine finger movements (e.g. walking, communicating, etc.) perfectly well. Some other tasks that I have always taken for granted are still possible but take extra time.
- *More realistic appraisal:* Although some things are more difficult for me at the moment, there are plenty of things that I can still do.

Arriving at a more realistic appraisal of the situation can make the distress more manageable; as the flowchart indicates, changing the appraisal of the situation will have an effect on our subsequent feelings and actions. Of course there will still be frustration and other emotions associated with the changed situation after a brain injury, but identifying and challenging thinking traps can sometimes make the difference between being able to cope with the distress and feeling overwhelmed by it.

Chapter 8

Communication, Planning Movements and Perception

Comments about material

These are three briefer presentations. This is not intended as a measure of their importance. Language is presented more briefly because by the nature of the common exclusion/-inclusion criteria for group work of this nature, those with marked communication difficulties (particularly receptively) may be better served by individual input, ideally in combination with a speech and language therapist. There is, of course, much profitable therapeutic group work aimed at people experiencing dysphasia, for which specialist speech and language therapist input is essential. In addition, whereas a topic such as attention can be divided for simplicity into three hierarchical levels, the complexities of language systems seem pragmatically harder to simplify to a level that will be accessible to a range of attendees within the confines of one session, beyond some of the basics such as distinguishing between expressive and receptive difficulties and verbal and non-verbal communication. There is less of a focus on the 'theory' and more of a focus on a range for practical suggestions from various sources, which will be of varying utility to people with different presentations.

As has been the approach in each chapter, only theoretical information that informs subsequent recommendations is included; as this single session is not intended to address any of the impairment-based interventions that speech and language therapists may choose to use, there is an accordingly briefer coverage of the 'theory'. Consideration is, however, given to some of the cognitive-communication difficulties that can arise.

Similarly, the common distinction between ideomotor and ideational dyspraxia is not explored in detail, although functional examples relate to both. This too reflects the overall trend in these chapters not to present theoretical information that does not inform the subsequent recommendations. As clinical intervention at present does not differ greatly between these two forms of dyspraxia, the distinction is not made explicit. There is support for this as a stance from Lezak (1995) who focuses more on the functional implications of an individuals' presentation. More recently, Goldstein (2004) concurs with such an approach.

Material to include

Communication

Slide 8.1

Communication difficulties are a common difficulty for people with neurological conditions. For example, about 20% of people who have had a stroke experience some difficulties with speech and language (Holland & Larimore, 2001). This can range from an occasional difficulty in finding the right word that you want to use, even though it feels like it's 'on the tip of your tongue', to much more severe difficulties that might make it almost impossible for someone to understand what is being said to them.

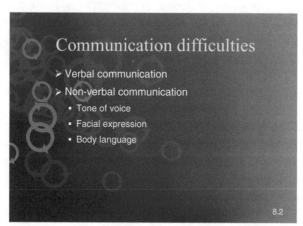

Slide 8.2

There is a wide range of ways in which we communicate with each other, and not all of them include using words. Tone of voice, facial expression and body language are examples of other ways of getting a message across. Often, however, it's difficulty with word-based communication that is most apparent and has the most obvious impact on interactions with other people, and there are some relevant points to make that may help us understand some of these difficulties and inform the way that we try and make communication easier.

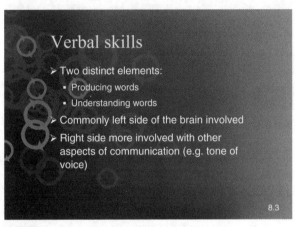

Slide 8.3

The first important distinction to make is between a difficulty with getting the words out and a difficulty with making sense of words that other people are saying. It's important to appreciate that they are two different skills, one related to understanding language and the other related to producing language. While it's not uncommon for people to have difficulties with both, it's vital that we don't assume that just because one of them is affected, the other is too. Just because someone has difficulty in expressing themselves verbally after, for example, a stroke, it doesn't automatically mean that they have difficulties with understanding what is said to them. One common trap that it's all too easy to fall into is to start talking to people like the stereotypical Englishman abroad, loudly and slowly, when they may have no difficulties comprehending us at all.

For most people it's the left side of the brain that is involved in producing and understanding spoken language, and if there is any injury or condition affecting the left hemisphere then difficulties with speech may be present. That doesn't mean that the other side of the brain isn't involved at all. It's generally thought that the right side of the brain plays an important part in some of the other aspects of communication, including tone of voice (for example, whether our voice goes up at the end of a question), and other associated factors, such as facial expression, eye contact, hand gestures and body language (McKenna, 2004). On some occasions, words aren't intended to be taken at face value; if someone arrives late for work and the boss says 'glad you could join us!', for example, it's crucial to the intended sense of the statement that someone can appreciate sarcasm and pick up non-verbal cues.

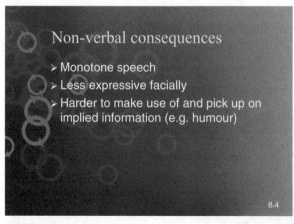

Slide 8.4

The implication of this is that people can experience changes that are subtler than struggling to find the words. These might include difficulties with speaking with a varied tone of voice or with the range of facial expressions or gestures that they normally would. This can come across as speaking in a monotone, or not seeming friendly or excited when speaking. It can appear as if the person is in fact depressed; that can sometimes be the case too, but it's important to consider whether subtle difficulties with expression are having an impact.

As well as impacting on how people speak, more subtle difficulties like this can have an impact on how well people understand information presented to them in the complicated world in which we live. For example, many television dramas rely on implying what might have happened, rather then spelling it out. For example, you might see someone being told some news and looking very shocked and distressed, so you would infer that the news was bad. That may be harder to deduce if it's more difficult to pick up on facial expression and tone of voice, so it might be harder to make sense of the plot of the programme. Similarly, much humour relies on implications, and complicated double meanings can be hard to appreciate.

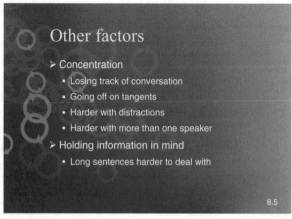

Slide 8.5

Communication and language don't happen in isolation from the other skills with which the brain is involved. Concentration, memory and planning can have marked impacts on how well a conversation might go, even if there are no specific difficulties with producing or understanding words. For example, if it's harder to maintain concentration because of something affecting the brain, then that's very likely to come across during a conversation. People commonly describe finding it harder to keep track of conversations, and maybe find their concentration drifting. This can be especially difficult if there is more than one person speaking at once, or in a pub with background music and noise. It is harder to concentrate when there are distractions, and even harder than that to keep track of two things at once, for example two friends expressing different opinions at the same time.

We all have a limit on how much information we can hold temporarily in our mind; for most people that's between five and seven chunks of information. Keeping that many pieces of information in mind is often crucial to understanding a particularly long sentence or instruction. After an injury involving the brain, sometimes it's only possible to hold maybe two or three pieces of information in mind at once while combining them and considering the meaning. That makes long sentences extra difficult to deal with.

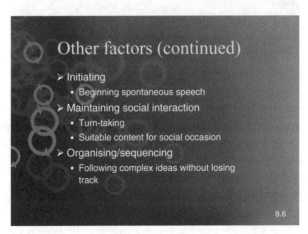

Slide 8.6

Some of the skills with which the front parts of the brain are involved are also relevant to communication. For example, we know that one job of the front parts of the brain is to 'initiate' behaviour, to act a bit like spark plugs in a car. If that isn't working so well, then it can mean that someone might find it more difficult to begin speaking and to have spontaneous conversations. There are other explanations for that of course, such as being in pain or discomfort or feeling depressed or angry, but it's worth considering whether difficulties with initiation may be playing a part. Similarly, we know that the front parts of the brain are very involved in monitoring behaviour and modifying our responses to situations. It can become more difficult to stick to the normal pattern of taking turns in conversation, and to keep the content of what is said suitable to the social situation. Similarly the frontal lobes are important in sequencing actions or ideas correctly, so it can be harder to follow through a complicated idea without going off the topic and losing track of the point being made. These kinds of difficulties that aren't immediately to do with understanding or producing words can often mean that there is a subtle change to the nature of interactions with people (Holland & Larimore, 2001).

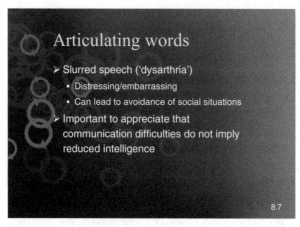

Slide 8.7

Another common difficulty that can have an impact on social interactions is a difficulty in articulating the words, which means that someone's speech sounds slurred. This is known to affect about a third of people after a head injury and is called 'dysarthria' (Holland & Larimore, 2001).

Whether the difficulty lies with being able to find the words that you want, being able to pronounce them clearly, or being able to follow what other people are saying in group settings, it can be extremely frustrating and distressing. In our society, so much of our identity and personality is expressed through the things we say, whether that be giving helpful advice to a friend, solving a difficult problem at work, or telling a joke at the dinner table, that communication difficulties can have an enormous impact on how people feel about themselves, and how they think that other people might feel about them. One of the common worries is for people to think that other people will assume that they are stupid because they are unable to express themselves so clearly or deal with lots of information presented to them at speed. It's important to remember that, just because there's inefficiency in one or more specific tasks with which the brain is involved (including producing words), this does not mean that there has been a general decrease in intelligence.

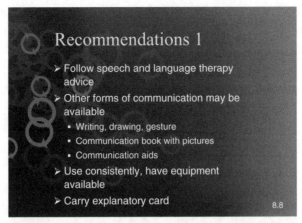

Slide 8.8

If someone is struggling to communicate using speech, it may be that they have been advised by a speech and language therapist to use other means of communication, be that writing, drawing, gesture or using a communication book with pictures, or another communication aid of some sort. If this has been advised, try and make full use of these strategies, and use them consistently. If it is helpful to use a pen and paper, for example, then these will need to be available for you to use at all times.

If people are unable to communicate using speech, then it can be a good idea to carry a card that explains this, which can be shown to people when you need to interact with them, as it can help them understand that you're certainly not less intelligent than before but have a specific difficulty with communication.

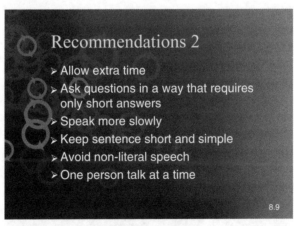

Slide 8.9

It may be that people speaking to someone with communication difficulties can take some of the burden off them, for example, by allowing them extra time to respond, or by asking questions in a way that requires only short answers. Speaking more slowly can help, as can keeping sentences short and simple. Avoiding using non-literal speech, such as metaphors and idioms, can reduce confusion. If there are several people involved in the conversation, try not to talk over one another.

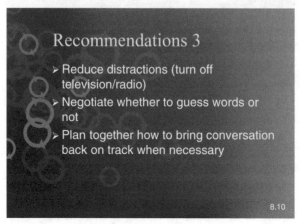

Slide 8.10

For both parties in a conversation there are some basic guidelines. Reducing distractions by, for example, turning off the television or radio, can be useful. Negotiating in advance whether or not the person struggling to find a word wants other people to try and guess it or not can be sensible, as some people hate having their sentences finished for them, while others find it a relief. It can also be a good idea to negotiate in advance how the individual would like to be informed that they have wandered off the topic of conversation, in a non-blaming and sensitive manner.

Planning movements

Slide 8.11

Some of the most immediately noticeable consequences of a condition affecting the brain are the physical effects, such as weakness down one side of the body or shakiness. In some cases, however, there can be some difficulties with making movements that are not related to physical weakness, but are more to do with how the brain plans to carry out the movement.

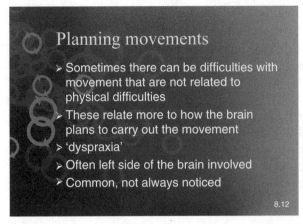

Slide 8.12

Examples might include using objects in the wrong way, for example picking up a toothbrush and using it like a razor, or having difficulty using a knife and fork to transfer food from a plate into your mouth. The technical term for these sorts of difficulties is 'dyspraxia', and it means that there is a difficulty with voluntary movement that isn't due to a physical difficulty or a lack of understanding of the task. It's often seen if a condition affects the left side of the brain, particularly an area very near to the areas involved in speech and language. Quite often difficulties with carrying out movements and communication difficulties will appear alongside each other.

Some estimates indicate that up to 80% of people who have had a stroke affecting the left side of the brain may have some of these difficulties in the early stages, and a year later, there's still up to 20% having such difficulties (Goldstein, 2004). It can sometimes be hard to spot though; often if people have a physical difficulty that affects, for example, one of their arms, by necessity they have to use the other hand. Any difficulties that they might be having with making movements might just be attributed to the fact that they're using the hand they don't normally use, rather than to a difficulty with planning movements.

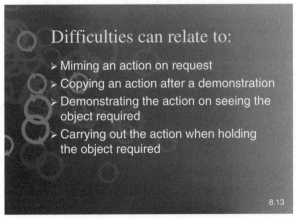

Slide 8.13

Sometimes the difficulties only show up when you're looking for them, and if that's the case then it's possible that in fact they have little impact on everyday life. It can be harder for someone to carry out a task when they're asked to; for example, 'can you show me how you'd comb your hair?' If that's difficult for someone, it may be that they're able to copy an action, so a demonstration or mime of carrying out the action will be enough to help them carry it out. Sometimes people will be able to carry out the action when they can see the object that they'd need, and sometimes people actually need to be holding the object before they can use it in the appropriate way. With that example, in daily life you usually would be holding the comb when you wanted to comb your hair, and so some difficulties at the earlier stages may go unnoticed and not be much of a concern.

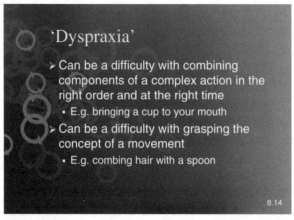

Slide 8.14

It can be the case that all the different components of a complex action are okay in themselves, but there is a difficulty with combining them in the right order (and at the right time) to make up the whole action. An example would be reaching to pick up a cup and bring it to your mouth. In this example, it may be that someone is well aware of what they intend to do, so their overall goal of having a drink is intact, but they can't achieve it because of the difficulty coordinating all the different stages. Alternatively, there can be difficulties with appreciating the concept of a movement, or the idea behind what an object is used for. This might result in, for example, combing one's hair with a spoon. This can have marked effects on everyday life, as a difficulty appreciating the use of objects like combs or razors can make personal care difficult to carry out independently. Sometimes very automatic movements are spared, such as waving goodbye in a social setting, although this is not always the case.

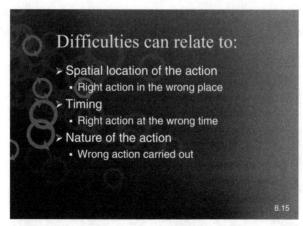

Slide 8.15

The different types of difficulties can be summarised as being either spatial (that is, the correct action performed but in the wrong place), temporal (that is, the correct action performed but at the wrong time) or content-related (the wrong action performed) (Rothi et al., 1997, cited in Goldstein, 2004). The left side of the brain is particularly involved in selecting which actions are going to be used to achieve a goal (Schluter et al., 2001), and that's why damage to the left side of the brain can lead to difficulties with any of these elements.

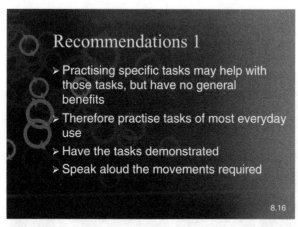

Slide 8.16

In terms of managing any of these difficulties, the familiar finding is that although practising a particular task will help people improve at carrying out that particular task, it won't generalise such that other tasks will see the benefit. The best advice is to practise those specific tasks that are of most everyday use to each individual, and as well as having the tasks demonstrated for you (which can be a help), it can sometimes help to speak aloud the movements, that is to verbalise what the planned movement is (Goldstein, 2004).

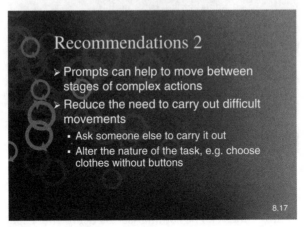

Slide 8.17

It can also help to have somebody prompting for each stage of the action. The other alternative is to try and reduce the need to carry out those movements that are difficult, by altering the nature of the task or asking someone else to do it for you. For example, for some people, not wearing clothes that have buttons on them might reduce the frustration associated with dressing, at little detriment to quality of life.

Perception

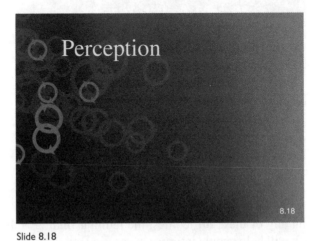

Slide 8.18

Skills related to vision and visual perception are massively important to us as humans going about our daily lives.

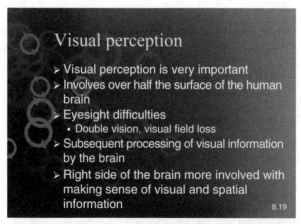

Slide 8.19

That's reflected by the amount of the brain that is dedicated to these skills; over half of the surface area of the brain is involved with vision and functions related to vision (Shaw, 2001). If difficulties do arise then it can have a marked impact on the ability to carry out activities of daily living.

There can be difficulties with basic eyesight after an injury to the brain or if there is a neurological condition; difficulties such as double vision or reduced visual fields are not uncommon. These aspects are fundamental to perceiving the world around us visually. Sometimes it's easy to attribute all difficulties with perception to problems with eyesight, but this is not always the case. Sometimes the difficulty lies with the brain's processing of information, for example if people become unable to recognise objects and fit them together in the way they want to (Humphreys & Riddoch, 1987). While the very back parts of the brain deal with the basic elements of visual perception, it's the right side of the brain that is involved with the more complex aspects of managing visual and spatial information.

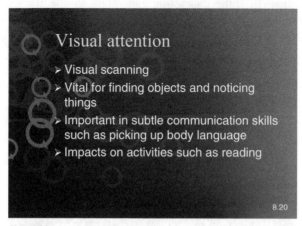

Slide 8.20

One fundamental aspect of making good visual sense of the world around us is related to concentration. Just as we have to pay attention to the things that we hear to keep track of them, we also have to pay attention to the things that we see. Efficient visual scanning means that we are able to be aware of the whole range of things that are presented to us, so that we can for example look along the shelves in a supermarket and pick out the one item that we are looking for. If there is a difficulty with visual attention, then this scanning can become less efficient and this can lead to difficulties with everyday tasks, such as finding things, noticing things such as subtle body language in other people, and also with reading which requires scanning words on the page.

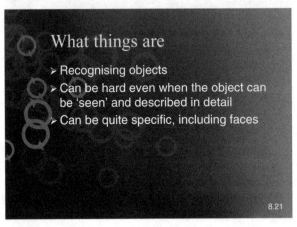

Slide 8.21

Beyond the fundamental requirements of adequate eyesight and visual scanning, there are two broad elements of perception that it is useful to consider. Essentially these relate to 'what things are' and 'where things are'. Knowing 'what something is' relates to object recognition. Sometimes people can have difficulty processing particular types of visual information such as colours or shapes. Sometimes people can have difficulty in recognising what a familiar object is, even though they can clearly describe it in terms of its physical characteristics. In some cases this can relate to specific categories of objects such as animals, or in some cases, people's faces, which can be very distressing for family members when it is harder for the person with such a difficulty to recognise them.

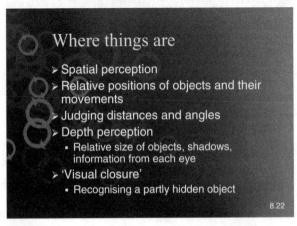

Slide 8.22

Knowing 'where something is' relates to spatial perception. This involves a complex range of skills that help us form accurate representations of the relative positions of objects and their movement relevant to each other and ourselves. This involves judging angles and judging distances, and also imagining how something would look if it was turned round. This is something we might take for granted when we're doing a jigsaw puzzle (will this piece fit if I rotate it?), and even more so when we're doing a routine daily activity such as putting our clothes on.

Depth perception plays a part in many of our interactions with the world around us, from picking up a cup of tea to driving a car. The skill of judging depth depends on coordinating information, such as the relative size of objects, making sense of shadows, and combining the slightly different information coming from each of the two eyes (Shaw, 2001).

One last specific skill to do with visuo-spatial functions is often called 'visual closure'. This refers to the skill of recognising an object when only part of it is visible to you. For example, if a book is partly hidden under a cushion then we can still recognise it as a book although we don't actually see the whole shape of it. If this skill is more difficult, it can make it harder for people to make use of the things around them with subsequent effects on how easy it is to carry out tasks such as personal care.

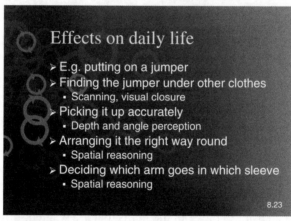

Slide 8.23

It is perhaps in the area of personal care that some of these difficulties first become apparent. The example of putting on a jumper makes the point that difficulties with visual or spatial perception can make the task very difficult to achieve. Firstly, the jumper might be half hidden under another item of clothing, so recognising it as a jumper might be more difficult in the first place if there's a difficulty with what we call 'visual closure'. Reaching to pick up the jumper involves some depth perception, some calculation of angles and direction, and some hand-eye coordination. Turning the jumper round so that it's positioned in the right way for us to put it on involves mentally rotating it until we recognise that it's the right way round and not back to front or inside out. There's the task of working out which arm needs to go in which sleeve, and the distance and angle to push the arm through. A difficulty with any of these stages can lead to marked problems with getting dressed. If there are such difficulties then there are marked safety implications for other everyday tasks such as crossing roads safely, let alone driving.

Finding our way around is another skill that can be made harder due to perceptual difficulties. It can be particularly hard to work out which way to go in a new setting. The sort of skills needed for this would involve picking up on cues such as signposts or landmarks, judging distances, and working out mentally how different roads or paths might join up, and imagining where you might end up if you were to take a turning.

The most useful approach is to try and compensate for any such difficulties rather than to try and restore the function. Although it won't lead to a general improvement in perceptual skills, practising a specific task will help with that task, so there is benefit to practising particular tasks that you may need to do every day such as those involved in washing or dressing.

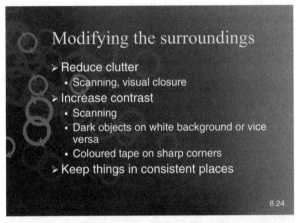

Slide 8.24

Modifying the surroundings can have benefits. The most basic advice is to reduce clutter, as this can make it easier to pick out the items that are wanted. If there is a lot of clutter in the background it can be harder to spot the desired object, either because of visual scanning difficulties, which are made worse by having lots of distractions present, or because of visual closure difficulties (if the object is partly covered up by something else it can be harder to identify).

Another suggestion is to try and increase the contrast of objects against their background, so that they stand out more and are harder to miss. For example, if the bathroom is mainly made up of white tiles, get a dark coloured toothbrush and razor. If the table is dark wood, try using white crockery and cutlery. If it's hard to find the brakes on the wheelchair, then wrap some brightly coloured tape around the handle. This approach can also be useful if there are any sharp corners that someone finds themselves frequently banging into because they don't notice them so easily (Shaw, 2001). Keeping things in consistent places wherever possible can also reduce difficulties.

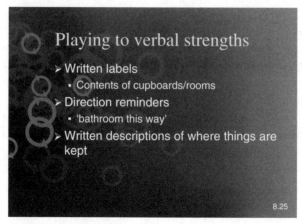

Slide 8.25

If verbal skills are just as good as ever, it can sometimes be useful to make use of written labels around the house, for example identifying what is in cupboards or which is the bedroom. Direction reminders can also be helpful, such as 'bathroom this way'. Similarly written descriptions of where things are kept can he helpful, for example 'shaving kit in bathroom cabinet'.

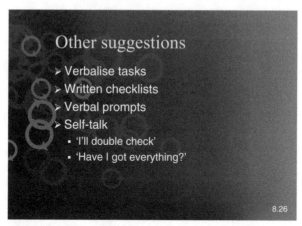

Slide 8.26

It is usually the right side of the brain that is most involved with visuo-spatial skills. If the right side of the brain has been affected, then it may be that the left side of the brain is just as good as ever and we can try and use some of its skills to reduce the effects of perceptual difficulties on daily activities. We know that the left side of the brain is very involved with language skills and handling verbal information. Sometimes it can help, therefore, to verbalise the task in hand, for example saying out loud 'hold the jumper with the label closest to me', or 'put the spoon into the sugar bowl'. For tasks with several stages, written checklists of instructions can be helpful, or alternatively spoken prompts from somebody else.

If someone has good awareness that their difficulties lie with visual scanning, then using 'self-talk' or 'self-instructional statements' can be a useful habit to acquire, for example 'I'll search again carefully', 'I'll double check', 'Am I doing this right?', or 'Have I got everything I need?'.

In summary, there can be a range of difficulties associated with visual or spatial organisation, and these can have an impact on activities of daily living. Making changes to the surroundings can be helpful, as can establishing habits of consciously double-checking and perhaps also verbalising tasks.

Communication

Communication difficulties are common for people with neurological conditions. Difficulties with speech and language can range from difficulties finding the word you want to use to having marked difficulty understanding what other people are saying. As well as words, other aspects of communication can be affected, including tone of voice, facial expression and use of body language. Slurred speech is also common.

Language difficulties can affect either the production of language (speaking or writing) or the understanding of language (comprehending spoken or written words) or both. Just because one aspect is more difficult does not mean that so is the other, and neither difficulty in itself necessarily reflects any decrease in general intelligence.

The left side of the brain is most commonly involved with verbal skills, while the right side is often involved with the other aspects of communication mentioned above. Although difficulties with words themselves can be more obvious, difficulties appreciating the meanings associated with tone of voice and facial expression also have effects on social interactions (for example, picking up on sarcasm or subtle implications that someone needs to finish the conversation).

Skills such as concentration, memory and planning are involved in communication, and difficulties with these skills can impact on conversations even when there may be no specific difficulties with language use. For example, it may be hard to keep track of a conversation, particularly if several people are speaking at once. It may be hard to follow a logical argument, as several pieces of information need to be kept in mind at once. It may be more difficult to stick to the usual 'turn-taking' structure of a conversation, and it may be harder to stick to the topic in hand without going off at tangents.

Advice from a speech and language therapist is very helpful in managing this range of difficulties. If particular aids to communication or exercises have been recommended, then using these consistently and making sure that you have any equipment you need are important.

Some people find it helpful to carry a card explaining their difficulties with communication in order to show people with whom they interact.

Basic recommendations for both parties in a conversation often include:

- Reducing distractions (turn off television/radio).
- Allow extra time for responses.
- Ask questions that require short answers.
- Speak a little more slowly.
- Keep sentences short and simple.

❑ Avoid using speech that isn't literal (e.g. sarcasm, metaphors).
❑ Try not to have more than one person speaking at once.

Planning Movements

Even when there is no physical weakness of the limbs, sometimes there can be problems with carrying out movements as intended because of a difficulty with how the brain plans to carry out the movement. This is called 'dyspraxia'.

The difficulty with planning movements can relate to organising the actions correctly, even when there is a clear idea of what the overall goal is; for example, picking up a cup and bringing it to your mouth may be difficult as there are several stages that need to be coordinated. Sometimes it is the idea of what an object is used for that presents the difficulty (e.g. knowing what to do with a comb).

Practising specific tasks may help with each particular task, but improvements don't often generalise. Practising the most relevant tasks for everyday life is recommended. Sometimes having the tasks demonstrated can help, as can speaking aloud what the movements required are or being prompted by someone else for each stage of a task.

It is sometimes possible to reduce the need to carry out particular tasks that are difficult, for example by choosing not to wear clothes that have buttons if doing up buttons is harder.

Perception

Over half of the surface area of the brain is involved with vision and visual perception. If the brain is injured in some way then there can be difficulties with eyesight itself, but also difficulties with the ways in which the brain deals with the visual information that is seen.

The brain is responsible for efficient visual scanning, which allows us to pay attention to the range of things that are visible to us. This scanning ability allows us to notice things and pick things out from complicated backgrounds, such as when we are searching for an item on a supermarket shelf. If there is a difficulty with this then it can be harder to notice things, pick up on subtleties such as body language, and carry out activities such as reading.

Sometimes there can be difficulties with recognising what objects are, and sometimes the difficulties lie with working out how objects relate to each other in space. Judgements such as this involve a range of skills, including depth perception, judging angles and distances and sometimes imagining how objects would look if they were the other way round. All these skills are involved in many everyday tasks, such as washing and dressing.

As well as having implications for personal care tasks, there can also be safety implications of perceptual difficulties. Crossing roads, driving and operating machinery can all become dangerous to yourself and other people if it is harder to make accurate perceptual decisions due to an injury to the brain.

Managing perceptual difficulties

Modifying the surroundings

1. Reducing clutter makes it easier to find items.
2. Increasing contrast of items against the background also makes items easier to spot (e.g. coloured key fobs).
3. Keeping things in consistent places means you will know where to find what you want.

Playing to verbal strengths

1. Verbalise the task (i.e. talk it through).
2. Use checklists and spoken/written prompts.
3. Use labels/direction signs around the house.
4. Use 'self-talk' (e.g. 'I'll search again carefully').

Chapter 9
Frequently Asked Questions

Some questions commonly arise during the course of information provision sessions. The following are some of the most common, and some brief information relating to them is presented for ease of access.

What about returning to work?

For many people with acquired brain injury or long-term neurological conditions there are realistic difficulties – either physical or cognitive – with returning to previous occupations. While, with the support of employers and colleagues, many of these can be compensated for, it does remain the case that many people are unable to resume the same level of employment. This is a very common consideration; one of the highest risk groups for acquired brain injury is young men, many of whom will be in employment at the time of the onset of their difficulties. For some occupations, difficulties such as slower information processing or difficulties maintaining concentration for extended periods of time will raise safety concerns, for example if the job involves a lot of driving. In other work settings, it will be possible to work around difficulties, with, for example, divided attention, by the implementation of some changes to the workspace. Some common recommendations for reducing difficulties in the workplace involve having a quiet area to work in and only having to manage one task at any one time.

Fatigue is very relevant when attempting a return to work. Fatigue is very common after a condition affecting the brain and can make tasks that involve any physical or mental exertion completely exhausting. For this reason, a graded return to work is the general recommendation, starting with perhaps only a couple of hours on some days in the week, and then gradually increasing the number of hours and the number of days as stamina allows. One danger with returning to work too soon after a mild head injury is that there will still be symptoms, such as headaches and concentration difficulties, that will limit the success of the return to work, possibly leading to loss of confidence, which can lead to further difficulties (Tyerman, 1996). Returning to work full-time before you are ready is generally counter-productive.

Some of the difficulties that can arise with, for example, executive function difficulties can only become apparent when faced with the level of challenge that is inherent in many work settings with their multiple demands and time pressures. As by their nature some of the executive difficulties can be hard for the person themselves to be fully aware of, it can be a useful idea to ask a trusted colleague to give you feedback about how you are managing the workload.

How can I manage fatigue?

Fatigue is an extremely common consequence of acquired brain injury and neurological conditions. It is far more than 'feeling a bit tired', and has been compared variously with 'a car suddenly running out of petrol', and 'feeling like the worst cold you've ever had'. It commonly means that tasks that were previously taken for granted become exhausting and necessitate long periods of rest afterwards. This commonly has a marked impact on home life, work and leisure settings. There is an effective way to tackle fatigue, which is called 'pacing'. Essentially, this reflects a 'little and often' approach, incorporating the recognition of the baseline level of activity that is currently feasible without reaching the point of exhaustion. This can be identified by experimentation; if it is apparent that 20 minutes of exertion leads to exhaustion for several days afterwards, then the baseline might be that there should be no more than 15 minutes of sustained exertion in one go. This should be followed by a rest period, after which it may well be possible to carry out a further period of activity.

There are two particular traps to avoid. The first is the temptation to do 'just another 10 minutes' when it feels like a good day. This will lead to reaching the threshold at which exhaustion sets in and confounds planned activities for the next few hours if not days. The second trap to avoid relates to managing bad days. The temptation on a bad day (for example, the day following a day when you have overdone it and attempted more than the baseline level of activity) is to do nothing at all but rest. What this means, however, is that on that day you will not be doing anything towards increasing or maintaining your stamina. The combination of the two traps can mean that you get into a repeating pattern of overdoing it followed by a few days of doing nothing. This means that you are continually becoming exhausted and then trying to recover. Overall, this cycle can make stamina levels decrease rather than increase. The trick is to stick within your recognised baselines of activity even on good days, and to do at least some activity, preferably your baseline, when you're having a bad day. This way your stamina will gradually increase, and over time the baseline level of activity that you can manage can gradually be increased. Such an approach is very relevant when considering returning to work, as attempting to take on too much without scheduled breaks is generally counter-productive.

How can I find out about which benefits I can claim?

There are benefits available for some people who have lasting difficulties related to acquired brain injury or a neurological condition. It can be helpful to seek advice from people with specialist knowledge regarding these. Useful first points of contact include the Citizens' Advice Bureau, and the local Social Services.

Some of the voluntary organisations or charities related to specific conditions may also be able to provide general information or give suggestions about who to contact in your area.

Where can I find out more about my condition?

For many conditions there are specific voluntary organisations or charities established to provide support and information. The following is a selection of some relevant websites:

Headway	www.headway.org.uk
Stroke Association	www.stroke.org.uk
Encephalitis	www.encephalitis.info
Multiple sclerosis	www.mssociety.org.uk
Parkinson's Disease	www.parkinsons.org.uk
Alzheimer's Disease	www.alzheimers.org.uk
Epilepsy	www.epilepsynse.org.uk
	www.epilepsy.org.uk
Carers	www.carersuk.org

How long will it take to recover?

After a sudden onset acquired brain injury, such as a stroke or a head injury, it is impossible to predict with certainty either the timescale or the extent of recovery that will occur. Various features have been used in attempts to make predictions, including the duration of loss of consciousness and the length of time from the accident until someone is able to make continuous memories again. While these can serve as indicators of the severity of the injury, it remains the case that for any individual it is hard to make predictions. For example, if someone hits their head and subsequently experiences some dizziness and concentration difficulties, then firm estimates of how long these will persist can not be made with any degree of accuracy.

Not uncommonly, people with acquired brain injury have been told at some stage in their treatment that their recovery may take up to six months or two years, and after that time no further recovery is to be expected. Such estimates, while giving the impression that it will not be a quick recovery, are often unhelpful. Firstly, it provides an often unrealistic impression that a full recovery of impairments is to be expected, and secondly, it flies in the face of the experience of many people who have sustained an acquired brain injury and continue to make slow progress some years after their injury (Meacham, 2005).

The most useful information to provide is the typical recovery curve (Chapter 3, slide 3.19), which indicates that there is often relatively rapid initial recovery, which slows down over an unspecified length of time. At some point, the recovery curve might plateau, or reduce to a very slow and gradual recovery. It is often only in hindsight that the stage of this graph that someone has reached can be appreciated. Even if the recovery curve does not reach previous levels of functioning (Chapter 3, slide 3.20), then functional improvement may still be made by adopting appropriate compensatory strategies that reduce the impact of persisting difficulties on daily life.

The rough graph hides the fact that there are likely to be periods of time when things go better than at other times during recovery, for various reasons including fatigue and mood, so the graph would realistically look less smooth and have more variations within it.

What about driving?

Any condition involving the brain can have implications for driving safely. Aside from physical difficulties that can make driving an unadapted car difficult, the range of difficulties covered in the previous chapters are also extremely relevant. Concentration is essential when driving, and if someone is more distractible then there are obvious safety concerns. Similarly, if people have more difficulty with concentrating on two things at once, this can be extremely dangerous in a situation that often requires awareness of several factors at any one time. If people take longer to process information, decide on a response and then put it into practice, then this can slow their reaction speed, which can be dangerous when driving. Any difficulties with visual skills, such as scanning the road ahead effectively, or judging distances, or judging how quickly another vehicle or pedestrian is moving, can also obviously be dangerous. As the consequences of driving when it may not be safe can literally be fatal, and affect other people as well as just the driver, it obviously needs to be considered carefully. It is important to inform the DVLA (Drivers Medical Group, DVLA, Swansea, SA99 1TU) of what has happened to you. It is the driver's legal responsibility to tell the DVLA of anything that may affect their ability to drive. Seeking your GP's advice about returning to driving is a good start, although they will not always have a full picture of the range of difficulties affecting you, and the final decision about fitness to drive rests with the DVLA. It may be that if some of the difficulties we have covered are relevant to you, you will be asked to undergo an assessment to make sure that you are not putting yourself or other people at risk by driving when it is not safe. The DVLA states that after a stroke, people cannot drive for at least one month.

What about brain plasticity?

One question that can arise relates to the mechanisms by which recovery may occur. Common lay beliefs involve 'other parts of the brain taking over' lost functions, or nerve cells re-growing. There is much current research going on into the field of neuroplasticity and neurogenesis in humans. At present, the evidence is that, while some neurogenesis may have been demonstrated in one particular part of the adult human brain (the hippocampus) (Eriksson et al., 1998), there are yet to be any clinical implications of this. No conclusions have been reached as to whether or not such cells are able to function adaptively, and indeed there remains some doubt as to whether or not the cells detected in such studies truly are new neurons or glial cells (Rakic, 2004). There is also little evidence supporting the notion that in adult humans the cognitive functions of damaged areas of the brain can be taken over by other parts of the brain. This certainly does not meant that functional recovery is not possible, but rather that it may be more parsimoniously attributed to (sometimes very subtle) compensatory behaviour, which makes use of intact pathways within the brain.

What, then, does underlie the recovery often seen in the early weeks following an acquired brain injury? Some of this can be attributable to some of the physical processes that occur after an injury to part of the brain. When some neurons die, then this can mean that there is some swelling in that area, and there can be changes to the blood flow to that part of the brain. There can also be toxins produced by the death of the cells. These factors can mean that the cells in the vicinity of the damaged cells can have their own functioning hampered although they have not been killed themselves. In addition, some of the cells that have been killed will have had connections with nearby surviving cells. All this means that the surviving cells may not be working in their ideal physical, chemical or electrical environment after the injury. Over time, however, some of these restricting features settle down. Swelling subsides, and the cells manage to compensate for changes to their connections and can change their sensitivity to inputs from other surviving cells. Their function can become optimised again, which can underlie some of the spontaneous recovery often seen after a brain injury. Processes such as this certainly do not entail the genesis of new neurons, but rather adaptations made by surviving neurons.

What are the benefits of setting goals?

The sessions described mention many strategies that may usefully be applied to reduce the day-to-day impact of ongoing cognitive difficulties. In order for them to have an effect, however, it can be helpful to make use of goal-setting techniques that will include some planning. The acronym SMART is commonly applied when setting goals such that they stand a chance of being implemented. This acronym refers to the features of a useful goal, in that it should be specific, measurable, achievable, realistic and timed. For example, rather than a vague intention to 'use a diary', a SMART goal would be 'to check the diary whenever your watch's hourly time signal goes off' and would necessitate the planned (possibly prompted) prior action of setting the watch's hourly chime, and making sure that the diary contains all the information it needs to (which may introduce a second goal that also needs to be SMART, i.e. when the diary will be updated and by whom).

SMART goals are realistic. This is an important consideration, for if people have unrealistic expectations of themselves then they are setting themselves up for disappointment and frustration when they are unable to achieve them. Setting goals that can be achieved, on the contrary, fosters a cycle of achievement and increased confidence, and over time brings functional benefits.

What can I do during the scheduled breaks in my fatigue management plan?

Learning how to relax carries a number of benefits. Not least it can be a useful way to manage stress and anger, but it can also be a useful skill when attempting to implement fatigue management strategies. Very often, one obstacle for people trying to adopt such strategies is knowing what to do during the frequently scheduled rest periods. Many activities that are suggested do in fact involve just as much physical or mental exertion as the main activity itself (such as reading or walking). One practical suggestion is to do some relaxation, as this can take an appropriate length of time to carry out thoroughly, such that it constitutes an effective break from the main task, and it is also inherently restful.

While there are many and varied approaches to relaxation, the two most commonly used key elements involve diaphragmatic breathing and progressive muscular relaxation. Any other elements, such as music or tapes, can be adopted by the individuals concerned if they find them helpful, or not if they don't. Rehearsing diaphragmatic breathing and progressive muscular relaxation can be a good use of time within one of the sessions if attendees are not familiar with them.

References

Aggleton, J.P. (1997). *Memory: a seminar for health professionals*. London: Mind Matters Seminars.

Ajzen, I. (1985). From intentions to actions: A theory of planned behaviour. In J. Kuhl & J. Beckman (Eds.), *Action control: from cognition to behaviour*. Berlin: Springer-Verlag pp. 11–39.

Astrom, M. (1996). Generalised anxiety disorder in stroke patients: A three-year longitudinal study. *Stroke, 27*, 270–275.

Barton, J., Levene, J., Kladakis, B. & Butterworth, C. (2002). Stroke: A group learning approach. *Nursing Times, 98(7)*, 34–35.

Beck, A.T. (1967). *Depression: clinical, experimental and theoretical aspects*. New York: Harper & Row.

Beck, A.T. (1976). *Cognitive therapy and the emotional disorders*. London: Penguin.

Bion, W.R. (1970). *Attention and interpretation*. London: Tavistock.

Blackburn, I.M. & Davidson, K.M. (1990). *Cognitive therapy for depression and anxiety: a practitioner's guide*. Oxford: Blackwell.

Blake, N., Burns, J. & van den Broek, M. (2005). What's in this for me? The patient's experience of neuropsychological assessment in the context of neurorehabilitation. Paper presented at Neuropsychological Rehabilitation Conference, July, National University of Ireland, Galway.

Boschen, K.A., Tonack, M. & Gargaro, J. (2003). Long-term adjustment and community reintegration following spinal cord injury. *International Journal of Rehabilitation Research, 26(3)*, 157–164.

Brain and Spine Foundation (2005). Update on information access project. *Brain and Spine Bulletin*, Summer/Autumn, 4.

Brooks, N., Campsie, L., Symington, C., Beattie, A. & McKinlay, W. (1986). The five-year outcome of severe blunt head injury: A relative's view. *Journal of Neurology, Neurosurgery & Psychiatry, 49(7)*, 764–770.

Brubaker, C. & Wickersham, D. (1990). Encouraging the practice of testicular self-examination: A field application of the theory of reasoned action. *Health Psychology, 9*, 154–163.

Callahan, C.D. (2001). The assessment and rehabilitation of executive function disorders. In B. Johnstone & H.H. Stonnington (Eds.), *Rehabilitation of neuropsychological disorders: a practical guide for rehabilitation professionals*. Hove: Psychology Press, pp. 87–124.

Champion, A.J., Higbed, L., Jones, K. & Thomson, A.S. (2005). *Evaluation of a single-session 'memory group' intervention*. Poster presentation (abstract number 496) at Neuropsychological Rehabilitation Conference, July, National University of Ireland, Galway.

Couldridge, L., Kendall, S. & March, A. (2001). A systematic overview – a decade of research. The information and counselling needs of people with epilepsy. *Seizure, 10(8)*, 605–614.

Cropley, M.L., MacLeod, A.K. & Tata, P. (2000). Memory retrieval and subjective probability judgements in control and depressed participants. *Clinical Psychology and Psychotherapy, 7*, 367–378.

Darragh, A.R., Sample, P.L. & Krieger, S.R. (2001). 'Tears in my eyes 'cause somebody finally understood': Client perceptions of practitioners following brain injury. *American Journal of Occupational Therapy, 55(2)*, 191–199.

Department of Health (2001). *The expert patient: A new approach to chronic disease management for the 21st century*. London: Department of Health.

Department of Health (2004). *Better information, better choices, better health: Putting information at the centre of health*. London: Department of Health.

Department of Health (2005). *National Service Framework for Long-term Conditions*. London: Department of Health.

Drummond, A.E.R. (1990). Leisure activities after stroke. *International Disability Studies, 12*, 157–160.

Drummond, A., Lincoln, N. & Juby, L. (1996). Effects of a stroke unit on knowledge of stroke and experiences of hospital. *Health Trends, 28*, 26–30.

Eriksson, P.S., Perfilieva, E., Bjoerk-Eriksson, T., Alborn, A.M., Nordborg, C., Peterson, D.A. & Gage, F.H. (1998). Neurogenesis in the adult human hippocampus. *Nature Medicine, 4(11)*, 1313–1317.

Evans, J.J. (2001). Rehabilitation of the dysexecutive syndrome. In R.Ll. Wood & T.M. McMillan (Eds.), *Neurobehavioural disability and social handicap following traumatic brain injury*. Hove: Psychology Press, pp. 209–227.

Evans, J. (2002a). *Neuropsychological assessment and rehabilitation: executive function and attention problems in neuropsychological rehabilitation*. Continuing Professional Development Series Workshop, May, University of Exeter.

Evans, J. (2002b). *Can impaired executive functions be restored or retrained?* Presentation at 'Effectiveness of Rehabilitation for Cognitive Deficits' Conference, September, Cardiff City Hall.

Evans, J. (2003). Disorders of Memory. In L.H. Goldstein & J.E. McNeil (Eds.), *Clinical neuropsychology: A practical guide to assessment and management for clinicians*. Chichester: Wiley, pp. 143–164.

Evans, R.L., Bishop, D.S. & Haselkorn, J.K. (1991). Factors predicting satisfactory home care after stroke. *Archives of Physical Medicine and Rehabilitation, 72*, 144–147.

Fleminger, S., Oliver, D.L., Williams, H.W. & Evans, J. (2003). The neuropsychiatry of depression after brain injury. *Neuropsychological Rehabilitation, 13*, 65–87.

Forster, A., Smith J., Young, J., Knapp, P., House, A. & Wright, J. (2002). Information provision for stroke patients and their caregivers (Cochrane review). In *The Cochrane Library, Issue 2*. Oxford: Update Software.

Freeman, J.A., Ford, H., Mattison, P., Thompson, A.J., Clark, F., Ridley, J., et al. (2002). *Developing MS healthcare standards: evidence-based recommendations for service providers*. London: The MS Society and the MS Professional Network.

Gariballa, S.E., Peet, S.M., Fotherby, M.D., Parker, S.G. & Castleden, C.M. (1996). The knowledge of hospital patients about vascular disease and their risk factors. *Postgraduate Medical Journal, 72*, 605–608.

Gillespie, D.C. (1997). Post-stroke anxiety and its relationship to coping and stage of recovery. *Psychological Reports, 80*, 1059–1064.

Glisky, E. (2002). *Treating memory impairment*. Presentation at 'Effectiveness of Rehabilitation for Cognitive Deficits' Conference, September, Cardiff City Hall.

Goldstein, L.H. (2004). Disorders of voluntary movement. In L.H. Goldstein & J.E. McNeil (Eds.), *Clinical neuropsychology: A practical guide to assessment and management for clinicians*. Chichester: Wiley, pp. 211–228.

Goldstein, L.H., Adamson, M., Jeffery, L., Down, K., Barby, T., Wilson, C., et al. (1998). The psychological impact of MND on patients and carers. *Journal of the Neurological Sciences, 160(1)*, s114–s121.

Gracey, F. (2002). Mood and affective problems after traumatic brain injury. *Advances in Clinical Neuroscience and Rehabilitation, 2(3)*, 18–19.

Hakim, E.A., Bakheit, A.M.O., Bryant, T.M., Roberts, M.W.H., McIntosh-Michaels, S.A., Spackman, A.J., et al (2004). The social impact of multiple sclerosis – a study of 305 patients and their relatives. *Disability and Rehabilitation, 22(6)*, 228–293.

Halligan, P.W. & Marshall, J.C. (1993). The history and clinical presentation of neglect. In I.H. Robertson & J.C Marshall (Eds.), *Unilateral neglect: clinical and experimental studies.* Hove: Lawrence Erlbaum Associates, pp. 3–25.

Hanger, H.C. & Mulley, G.P. (1993). Questions people ask about stroke. *Stroke, 24(4)*, 536–538.

Hayes, N.M. & Coetzer, R. (2003). Developing a brain injury service information booklet based on service users' perceived needs. *Clinical Psychology, 21*, 36–38.

Headway: the Brain Injury Association (2005). The shock of a brain injury survivor. *Promotional Letter*, 19/08/05.

Heiman, P. (1950). On counter transference. *International Journal of Psychoanalysis, 31*, 81–84.

HMSO (1999). *White paper. Saving lives: Our healthier nation.* London: HMSO.

Holland, D. & Larimore, C. (2001). The assessment and rehabilitation of language disorders. In B. Johnstone & H.H. Stonnington (Eds.), *Rehabilitation of neuropsychological disorders: a practical guide for rehabilitation professionals.* Hove: Psychology Press, pp. 161–194.

Hounsa, A.M., Godin, G., Alihonou, E. & Valois, P. (1993). An application of Ajzen's theory of planned behaviour to predict mothers' intention to use oral rehydration therapy in a rural area of Benin. *Social Science & Medicine, 37*, 253–261.

Humphreys, G.W. & Riddoch, M.J. (1987). *To see but not to see.* London: Lawrence Erlbaum Associates.

Jacobs, H.E. (1988). Los Angeles head injury survey: Procedure and initial findings. *Archives of Physical Medicine and Rehabilitation, 69*, 425–431.

Johnson, J., Smith, P. & Goldstone, P. (2001). *Evaluation of MS specialist nurses: A review and development of the role, executive summary.* London: Southbank University and MS Research Trust.

Johnston, K. & Maidment, R. (2004). Carers' understanding of Alzheimer's disease. *The Psychologist, 17(10)*, 593.

Kalra, L., Evans, A., Perez, I., Melbourn, A., Patel, A., Knapp, M., et al. (2004). Training carers of stroke patients: Randomised controlled trial. *British Medical Journal, 328*, 1099–1011.

Kelly-Hayes, M. & Paige, C. (1995). Assessment and psychological factors in stroke rehabilitation. *Neurology, 45(2)*, Supplement 1, s29–s45.

Kendall, S., Thompson, D. & Couldridge, L. (2004). The information needs of carers of adults diagnosed with epilepsy. *Seizure, 13(7)*, 499–508.

Kennedy, P. & Rogers, B.A. (2000). Anxiety and depression after spinal cord injury: A longitudinal analysis. *Archives of Physical Medicine and Rehabilitation, 81*, 932–937.

Kersten, P., Low, J., Ashburn, A., George, S. & McLellan, D. (2002). The unmet needs of young adults who have had a stroke: Results of a national UK survey. *Disability and Rehabilitation, 24*, 860–866.

Khan-Bourne, N. & Brown, R.G. (2003). Cognitive behaviour therapy for the treatment of depression in individuals with brain injury. *Neuropsychological Rehabilitation, 13*, 89–107.

King, N.S. (2003). Post-concussion syndrome: Clarity amid the controversy? *British Journal of Psychiatry, 183*, 276–278.

King's Fund (1988). King's Fund Forum Consensus Statement: The treatment of stroke. *British Medical Journal, 297,* 126–128.

Kite, S., Jones, K. & Tookman, K. (1999). Specialist palliative care and patients with non-cancer diagnoses: The experience of a service. *Palliative Medicine, 13(6),* 477–484.

Knight, R.G., Devereux, R. & Godfrey, H.P.D. (1998). Caring for a family member with a traumatic brain injury. *Brain Injury, 12(6),* 467–481.

Levitt, T. & Johnstone, B. (2001). The Assessment and rehabilitation of Attention Disorders. In B. Johnstone & H.H. Stonnington (Eds.), *Rehabilitation of neuropsychological disorders: A practical guide for rehabilitation professionals.* Hove: Psychology Press, pp. 27–32.

Ley, P. (1988). *Communicating with patients: Improving communication, satisfaction and compliance.* London: Croom Helm.

Lezak, M.D. (1995). *Neuropsychological assessment,* third edn. New York: Oxford University Press.

Liamaki, G. & Bach, L. (2003). Group intervention for carers of brain injured relatives: Thoughts and suggestions. *Clinical Psychology, 26,* 28–31.

Loftus, E.F. (1979). *Eyewitness testimony.* Cambridge MA: Harvard University Press.

Luria, A.R. (1963). Recovery of function after brain injury. New York: MacMillan.

Maitz, E.A. & Sachs, P.R. (1995). Treating families of individuals with traumatic brain injury from a family systems perspective. *Journal of Head Trauma Rehabilitation, 10(2),* 1–11.

Malec, J.F., Smigielski, J.S., Depompolo, R.W. & Thompson, J.M. (1993). Outcome evaluation and prediction in a comprehensive, integrated post-acute out-patient rehabilitation programme. *Brain Injury, 7,* 15–29.

Mant, J., Carter, J., Wade, D.T. & Winner, S. (1998). The impact of an information pack on patients with stroke and their carers: A randomised controlled trial. *Clinical Rehabilitation, 12,* 465–476.

Martin, K. & Aggleton, J.P. (1993). Contextual effects on the ability of divers to use decompression tables. *Applied Cognitive Psychology, 7,* 311–316.

McKenna, P. (2004). Disorders of language and communication. In L.H. Goldstein & J.E. McNeil (Eds.), *Clinical neuropsychology: A practical guide to assessment and management for clinicians.* Chichester: Wiley, pp. 165–184.

Meacham, C. (2005). Chief Executive's message. *Different Strokes Newsletter,* Number 28, 1.

Mesulam, M.M. (1985). Attention, confusional states and neglect. In M.M. Mesulam (Ed.), *Principles of behavioural neurology.* Philadelphia, PA: F.A. Davies.

Moniz-Cook, E. & Rusted, J. (2004). Neurorehabilitation strategies for people with neurodegenerative conditions. In L.H. Goldstein & J.E. McNeil (Eds.), *Clinical Neuropsychology: A practical guide to assessment and management for clinicians.* Chichester: Wiley, pp. 405–420.

Moorey, S. (1996). When bad things happen to rational people: Cognitive therapy in adverse life circumstances. In P.M. Salkovskis (Ed.), *Frontiers of cognitive therapy.* New York: Guilford Press, pp. 450–469.

Morrison, V.L., Johnston, M., MacWalter, R.S. & Pollard, B.S. (1998). Improving emotional outcomes following acute stroke: A preliminary evaluation of a work-book based intervention. *Scottish Medical Journal, 43(2),* 52–53.

Moscovitch, M. (1992). Memory and working-with-memory: A component process model based on modules and central systems. *Journal of Cognitive Neuroscience, 4(3),* 257–267.

Myers, L. & Abraham, A. (2005). Beyond 'doctor's orders'. *The Psychologist, 18(11),* 680–683.

NICE (2003). *Multiple Sclerosis: National clinical guidelines for diagnosis and management in primary and secondary care.* London: National Institute for Clinical Excellence/National Collaborating Centre for Chronic Conditions.

NICE (2005). *Post-traumatic stress disorder (PTSD): The management of PTSD in adults and children in primary and secondary care. Quick Reference Guide, Clinical Guideline 26.* London: National Institute for Clinical Excellence/National Collaborating Centre for Mental Health.

Nicholl, C.R.O., Lincoln, N.B., Francis, V.M. & Stephan, T.F. (2001). Assessment of emotional problems in people with multiple sclerosis. *Clinical Rehabilitation, 15,* 657–668.

Oddy, M., Humphrey, M. & Uttley, D. (1978). Subjective impairment and social recovery after closed head injury. *Journal of Neurology. Neurosurgery & Psychiatry, 41,* 611–661.

Oddy, M., Coughlan, A., Tyerman, A. & Jenkins, D. (1985). Social adjustment after closed head injury: A further follow-up seven years after injury. *Journal of Neurology, Neurosurgery and Psychiatry, 48,* 564–568.

O'Hara, L., Cadbury, H., De, S.L. & Ide, L. (2002). Evaluation of the effectiveness of professionally guided self-care for people with multiple sclerosis living in the community: A randomised controlled trial. *Clinical Rehabilitation, 16(2),* 119–128.

O'Mahoney, P.G., Rodgers, H., Thomson, R.G., Dobson, R. & James, O.F.W. (1997). Satisfaction with information and advice received by stroke patients. *Clinical Rehabilitation, 11,* 68–72.

Pace, G.M., Schlund, M.W., Hazard-Haupt, T., Christensen, J.R., Lashno, M., McIver, J., et al. (1999). Characteristics and outcomes of a home and community based neurorehabilitation programme. *Brain Injury, 13,* 535–546.

Parasuraman, R. (1998). *The attentive brain.* London: MIT Press.

Pardo, J.V., Fox, P.T. & Raichle, M.E. (1991). Localisation of a human system for sustained attention by positron emission tomography. *Nature, 349,* 61–64.

Park, N. (2002). *Treating attention impairments: A review of the evidence.* Presentation at 'Effectiveness of Rehabilitation for Cognitive Deficits' Conference, September, Cardiff City Hall.

Parkin, A.J. (1999). *Memory: a guide for professionals.* Chichester: Wiley.

Powell, J., Heslin, J. & Greenwood, R. (2002). Community based rehabilitation after severe traumatic brain injury: A randomised controlled trial. *Journal of Neurology, Neurosurgery and Psychiatry, 72(2),* 193–202.

Powell, T. (1994). *Head injury: A practical guide.* Bicester: Speechmark.

Powell, T. (2005). *Do beliefs about rehabilitation based upon the theory of planned behaviour predict engagement?* Paper presented at Neuropsychological Rehabilitation Conference, July, National University of Ireland, Galway.

Rakic, P. (2004). Immigration denied. *Nature, 427,* 685–686.

Raskin, S.A., Borod, J.C. & Tweedy, J. (1990). Neuropsychological aspects of Parkinson's disease. *Neuropsychology Review, 3,* 185–222.

Reynolds, M. (1978). No news is bad news: Patients' views about communication in hospital. *British Medical Journal, 1(6128),* 1673–1676.

Riley, G. (2005). *Threat appraisals and the avoidance of activities after TBI.* Paper presented at Neuropsychological Rehabilitation Conference, July, National University of Ireland, Galway.

Robertson, I.H. & Murre, J.M.J. (1999). Rehabilitation of brain damage: Brain plasticity and principles of guided recovery. *Psychological Bulletin, 125,* 544–575.

Robertson, I.H., Mattingley, J.B., Rorden, C. & Driver, J. (1998). Phasic alerting of neglect patients overcomes their spatial deficits in visual awareness. *Nature, 395,* 169–172.

Robertson, I.H., Ward, A., Ridgeway, V. & Nimmo-Smith, I. (1994). *Test of everyday attention.* Bury St Edmunds: Thames Valley Test Company.

Roland, M. & Dixon, M. (1989). Randomised controlled trial of an educational booklet for patients presenting with back pain in general practice. *Journal of the Royal College of General Practitioners, 39,* 244–246.

Rose, D. & Johnson, D. (1996). Brains, injuries and outcome. In F.D. Rose & D.A. Johnson (Eds.), *Brain injury and after: towards improved outcome.* Chichester: Wiley, pp. 1–20.

Ross, L. (1977). The intuitive psychologist and his shortcomings: Distortions in the attribution process. *Advances in Experimental Social Psychology, 10,* 173–220.

Roth, A.D. & Fonagy, P. (1996). *What works for whom? A critical review of psychotherapy research.* New York: Guilford Press.

Rothi, L.J.G., Raymer, A.M. & Heilman, K.M. (1997). Limb praxis assessment. In L.J.G. Rothi & K.M. Heilman (Eds.), *Apraxia: the neuropsychology of action.* Hove: Psychology Press, pp. 61–73.

Royal College of Physicians (1998). *Disabled people using hospitals: A charter and guidelines.* London: Royal College of Physicians.

Rutter, D.R. (2000). Attendance and reattendance for breast cancer screening: A prospective three-year test of the theory of planned behaviour. *British Journal of Health Psychology, 5(1),* 1–13.

Sackett, D.L. & Snow, J.C. (1979). The magnitude of compliance and noncompliance. In R.B. Haynes, D.W. Taylor & D.L. Sackett (Eds.), *Compliance in health care.* Baltimore, MD: Johns Hopkins University Press.

Schluter, N.D., Krams, M., Rushworth, M.F.S. & Passingham, R.E. (2001). Cerebral dominance for action in the human brain: The selection of actions. *Neuropsychologia, 39,* 105–113.

Schmahmann, J.D. & Sherman, J.C. (1998). Cerebellar affective syndrome. *International Review of Neurobiology, 41,* 433–440.

Shaw, J. (2001). The Assessment and rehabilitation of visual-spatial disorders. In B. Johnstone & H.H. Stonnington (Eds.), *Rehabilitation of neuropsychological disorders: A practical guide for rehabilitation professionals.* Hove: Psychology Press, pp. 125–160.

Sinnakaruppan, I. & Williams, D.M. (2001). Family carers and the adult head-injured: A critical review of carers' needs. *Brain Injury, 15,* 653–672.

Spence, C. & Driver, J. (2000). Attracting attention to the illusory location of a sound: reflexive crossmodal orienting and ventriloquism. *Neuroreport, 11(9),* 2057–2061.

Tasienski, T., Bergstrom, E. Savic, G., Gardner, B.P., Kennedy, P., Ash, D., et al. (2000). Sport/recreation and education/employment following spinal cord injury – a multi-centre study. *Spinal Cord, 38,* 173–184.

Temple, C. (1993). *The brain: an introduction to the psychology of the human brain and behaviour.* London: Penguin.

Thompson, P.J. & Corcoran, R. (1992). Everyday memory functions in people with epilepsy. *Epilepsia, 33*(supplement 6), S18–20.

Turner-Stokes, L. (2003). *Rehabilitation following acquired brain injury: National Clinical Guidelines.* London: British Society of Rehabilitation Medicine/Royal College of Physicians.

Tyerman, A. (1996). The social context. In F.D. Rose & D.A. Johnson (Eds.), *Brain injury and after: towards improved outcome.* Chichester: Wiley, pp. 97–117.

van Zomeren, A.H. & Brouwer, W.H. (1994). *Clinical neuropsychology of attention.* New York: Oxford University Press.

Weddell, R., Oddy, M. & Jenkins, D. (1980). Social adjustment after rehabilitation: A two year follow-up of patients with severe head injury. *Psychological Medicine, 10,* 257–263.

Weiner, B. (1980). A cognitive (attribution)-emotion-action model of helping behaviour: An analysis of judgments of help giving. *Journal of Personality and Social Psychology, 39,* 186–200.

Wellwood, I., Dennis, M.S. & Warlow, C.P. (1994). Perceptions and knowledge of stroke amongst surviving patients with stroke and their carers. *Age and Ageing, 23*, 293–298.

White, M. & Epston, D. (1990). Externalising of the problem. *Narrative means to therapeutic ends*. London: Norton, pp. 38–76.

Wilson, B.A. (1987). *Rehabilitation of memory*. London: Guilford Press.

Wilson, B.A. (2002). Towards a comprehensive model of cognitive rehabilitation. *Neuropsychological Rehabilitation, 12*, 97–110.

Wilson, B.A. & Moffat, N. (1992). *Clinical management of memory problems*, second edn. London: Chapman & Hall.

Wyer, S., Earll, L, Joseph, S., Giles, M. & Johnston, M. (2001) Increasing attendance at a cardiac rehabilitation programme: an intervention using the Theory of Planned Behaviour. *Coronary Health Care, 5*, 1–6.

Young, J. (2004). A randomised trial to evaluate improved routine communication to patients and carers after stroke. *The Research Findings Register*, Summary number 1288. Retrieved 26 May, 2005 from http://www.ReFeR.nhs.uk/ViewRecord.asp?ID=1288.

Zarit, S.H. & Edwards, A.B. (1999). Family caregiving: Research and clinical intervention. In R.T. Woods (Ed.), Psychological problems of ageing. Chichester: Wiley, pp. 153–193.

Index